The P~~~~~e

A powerful ~~~~~

day trad~~~ ~~ethod

Gabriele Fabris

The Price in Time
Copyright © 2023 Gabriele Fabris
All Rights Reserved.

ISBN: 9781096868576

Disclaimer

The opinions expressed in this text are in no way intended to constitute an invitation to engage in any transaction involving the purchase or sale of shares, futures contracts, stock options, funds or any other financial instruments. Therefore, they do not in any way constitute a public solicitation of savings or investment advice. The risks of loss from trading can be very high. Investors should carefully consider the risks involved in trading and investing on the basis of their financial situation. This presentation is for educational and informational purposes only, all the operations described are carried out in demo mode for educational purposes and are presented as a simple opportunity for reflection. By reading the contents, you acknowledge your responsibility in the use of the information and you agree to consult a professional financial advisor before any use or implementation of the information.

" The biggest problem with graphic analysis is self-illusion. Most of the time traders are convinced that a pattern is bullish or bearish based on their willingness to buy or sell. "

(Alexander Elder)

@gabry_trader_fx

The Price In Time Forex Strategy

Index

Introduction **15**

Understanding the charts **19**

Opening and closing times **25**

Sessions and times **29**

    Asian Session *30*

    European Session *31*

    American Session *32*

Price dynamics **33**

"Abnormal" days **41**

The importance of the opening price **47**

Determining the NTZ area **53**

Entry point **57**

Where to place Stop Loss and why **59**

Take Profit levels **61**

Supports and Resistances **65**

Fibonacci tips **69**

The NTZ boxes 77

The natural cycle of ranges 85

The timeframe does not count 91

The trading plan 97

Checklist 105

Money management 107
    Money management 109
    Risk management / Position sizing 113
    Risk reward 117

Trade management 121
    Model 1 122
    Model 2 125
    Model 3 131

How to handle the second pending order 135
    Variant A 137
    Variant B 138
    Variant C 139

The importance of backtesting 143

Final notes 145

Resources 149
    NTZ Box Breakout Indicator 151
    Customize the first 3 parameters 152
    Viewing the Spread 153

Money Manager *155*

Box of the Asian session *157*

Green Box (NTZ Range) *159*

Customize the appearance of the indicator *161*

Introduction

Hello,

My name is Gabriele Fabris, I am an independent trader born in Italy just outside Milan, I have been trading since 2006 and thanks to this inquisitiveness that has always made me stand out, I have come to discover the fascinating world of financial markets by turning trading into my core business.

In this book, I will present to you the knowledge I have acquired after years of research and study, by demonstrating how - after a thorough observation of the charts - I have come to understand that **the dynamics of price are repeated every day** and with these, I have come to develop the trading strategy that I have used for years, a well-defined working method that enables me to earn constantly in the financial markets.

Needless to say, how many hours - days and nights - I've spent on the charts looking spasmodically for the **"perfect pattern",** the one that enables you to generate constant gains over time. After years of studies and comparisons with very good traders, I have come to a certain conclusion: **the perfect patterns do not exist!**

And it is from this concept that the strategy ***The Price in Time*** was conceived.

A simple and effective technique in which I will show you:

- ✔ The right moment to enter the market
- ✔ Where to place stop loss and take profit
- ✔ The correct management of the trade
- ✔ How to protect your profits and limit your losses
- ✔ The most suitable position sizing and money management

The real benefit of ***The Price in Time*** strategy is its **non-discretionary nature**. A clear, consistent and well organized method **that will allow you to know exactly how to act in complete safety** and without any doubt, both when the market is in your favour and when the market is against you, because in both cases you will be supported by the results obtained in your backtest and consequently you will have full confidence in your future operations.

Why am I talking about complete safety? Because **the backtests** you do will be **based on two fundamental factors**, two elements that leave no room for discretion: **Price and Time**. Thanks to the price quotations in a given period of time, **you can analyze and test with certainty the past performances** so that you can determine the best choice for the future, that is the most suitable trade management to be applied to each individual instrument that you want to trade.

With ***The Price in Time*** strategy you don't have to spend hours in front of the charts to try to find all the various patterns of technical analysis - the most common flags, pennants, heads and shoulders and so on - that in my opinion leaves too much room for discretion, but you just have to turn on the PC and place your *buy* and *sell* orders and wait to enter the market knowing in advance how you will manage your trade. All this, without jumping from one time frame to another looking for the conviction that the pattern you have identified is really perfect and not the result of your conviction. Simple, isn't it?

Let me give you an example:

Let's take ten traders and ask them to analyze EUR/USD by applying the famous "head and shoulders" for the whole of 2016 and 2015; then let's ask them to simulate their trades based on this pattern. What would happen? A lot of confusion! We would certainly have ten different analyses and ten different operational performances.

So the question you have to ask yourself is:

How can I be sure it will be profitable in the long term if I'm not sure I'm basing my research on objective analysis criteria?

The answer **lies in the heart** of ***The Price in Time*** strategy: **analyzing markets based on objective and non-subjective criteria**, established with absolute clarity and precision, where confusion and uncertainty have no place, such that our ten traders will be able to consistently respond that EUR/USD performed the same for all in 2016 and 2015. All with the same analysis and performance, because the results will be due to the pure performance of the market and not due to the discretion of the trader. This means trading professionally!

I want you to know a little bit about me before I get to work.

Until a few years ago I would never have believed I would be capable of sharing this trading method of mine in such detail, which has matured from so much study, research and dedication, a method which I believe to be the spearhead of all my strategies; but, thanks to technology, I have recognized the fact that we now live in an increasingly "social" world, where everything is shared on the web and where I myself, thanks to others who shared has received precious help and infinite ideas and insights without which I would never have been able to create this trading method.

This is precisely why I decided to write this book: I want to give my own personal contribution both to those who are already experienced traders and to those who are simply smattering and are still trying to find their way.

My mission in this book is to give you a reflective, simple and practical idea so that you - like me - can find a trading style that suits your personality, a style that will allow you to feel comfortable every day in the financial markets with a profitable future.

Come on... it's time to get to work!

Understanding the charts

In all my years of trading I have mainly had to deal with three different schools of thought.

1. Traders loyal to any kind of indicators and oscillators (Figure 1).

Figure 1

2. Traders loyal to the most meticulous technical analysis (Figure 2).

Figure 2

3. Traders who support the so-called "naked" charts that analyze the markets through the search for candlestick patterns (Figure 3).

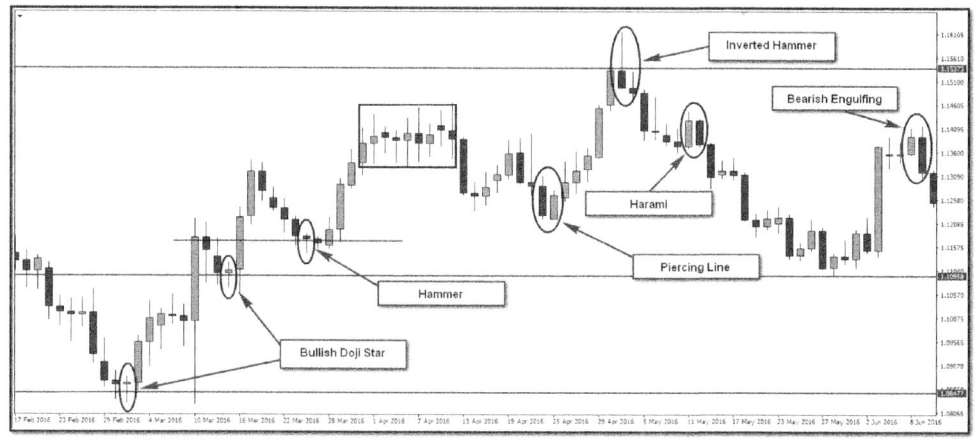

Figure 3

These trading methods - which are disclosed as profitable methods - are applied to our operations on the trust of what we are told, without taking the trouble to verify whether they can really be considered profitable in the long run. Most traders open a chart and make it slide backwards, by looking for the crossing of the moving averages, the stochastic inversion, the bullish triangle, the candlestick pattern and so on... "I would have entered here, I would have gone out here, there was the stop loss here, yes... ok, the strategy works!". All this with the conviction that a gain will certainly be made on the financial markets - the entire world of training says that such techniques work - they should be trusted no matter what.

Is this true?

Unfortunately, it's not a question of whether it works or not. It should be considered that if it is true that market movements are repetitive, to understand the future it is appropriate to first study the past. But a search carried out through a series of historical data, albeit very accurate, can not be considered reliable if carried out with a principle of discretion that varies from trader to trader.

That is why I believe that the more accurate our research into historical data is, the more effective our strategy will be. And to make this happen, we need to learn how to identify specific reference points in charts - points that are created by price movements within certain time bands - that give us the opportunity to base our analysis of historical data on objective data, without any independent interpretation, thus starting to use a real compass to orient ourselves in the great ocean of charts.

Once we have identified these time bands, we can begin to do the first backtests with absolute precision and obtain, firstly, a list of changes that correspond positively to the search criteria and secondly to make a pre-selection of the changes that in our opinion are more promising depending on the strategy.

We know that charts are a representation of **price** activity (vertical axis) over **time** (horizontal axis) (Figure 4). Price and time, in fact, are all that is necessary to go and determine the non-discretionary points on which to go and build our strategy.

Figure 4

If you've noticed, the charts I showed you in Figures 1, 2 and 3 all have one thing in common: the time factor is missing. Time is not intended as a timeframe but as the moment when the old trading day ends and the new one begins.

This is a very important element that should be taken into account when analyzing any chart, because it is the first non-discretionary reference point that gives us the opportunity to make a distinction between the various trading sessions.

Opening and closing times

Taking into account, the time factor on the chart to distinguish the different trading sessions means simply displaying the day separators. It may seem like a trivial concept, but during my experience as a trader I have seen a lot of - too many - people trading intraday without even knowing when a day in Forex officially ends, that is, when a daily candle closes on the chart and another one opens.

Forex is the world's largest financial market and is open 24 hours a day, 5 days a week, Monday to Friday; however, depending on where you are in the world, days and times may differ due to time zone and daylight savings time.

Generally the opening and closing times of the markets are indicated considering the GMT (Greenwich Mean Time), but you have to pay attention to the fact that, in the various periods of the year, each country can have different time zones. Frankfurt, for example, is at GMT+1 in winter and at GMT+2 when summer time comes.

In the following table I have summarized the opening and closing times of the Forex market in the various countries, considering the GMT time zone.

City	Time Zone	Opening Week	Closing Week
Auckland (Australia)	GMT +12	Monday at 10:00	Saturday at 10:00
Sydney (Australia)	GMT +10	Monday at 8:00	Saturday at 8:00
Tokio (Japan)	GMT +9	Monday at 7:00	Saturday at 7:00
Hong Kong (China)	GMT +8	Monday at 6:00	Saturday at 6:00
Bangkok (Thailand)	GMT +7	Monday at 5:00	Saturday at 5:00
Frankfurt (Germany)	GMT +1	Sunday at 23:00	Friday at 23:00
London (UK)	GMT	Sunday at 22:00	Friday at 22:00
New York (U.S.A.)	GMT -5	Sunday at 17:00	Friday at 17:00

Figure 4.1

In fact, the opening hours of the week begin with the opening of the stock exchange in Sydney on Monday morning at 10:00 local time (GMT+12), which coincides in London with Sunday evening at 22:00 (GMT); while the closing times of the week coincide with the closing of the New York Stock Exchange on Friday afternoon at 17:00 local time (GMT-5), which in turn coincides with Friday evening in London at 22:00 (GMT).

Similarly, again referring to the GMT time (London), at 21:59 on each day of the week we have the end of the day and at 22:00 the start of the new one (Figure 5); which means that on the platform we will see the closure of the old daily candle and the opening of the new one.

Figure 5

A specification is a must for the Metatrader platform (MT4): MT4 is the most popular platform for Forex trading; the servers are set to GMT +2, so on the MT4 charts we will see the day separators indicate 00:00 hours.

These concepts may seem obvious to some, but it is very important, regardless of the platform in use, to know the exact time shown by our chart compared to the GMT in London.

In fact, you should know that many of the platforms offered by brokers - and especially the Metatrader - do not have the option to change the GMT from the settings. Consequently, you should pay close attention to the time displayed on the charts because it is not always the same as the GMT time and since for the purposes of the strategy is essential to know the opening and closing times of the various sessions that make up the day, if we are misled by the "wrong" time of the platform our analysis on the historical data would be wrong, and consequently so would our trading.

As you can see in the red circle in Figure 6, when the day ends and the daily candle closes, the day separator shows the 00:00 hours, which actually corresponds to 22:00 GMT.

Figure 6

*As you read this book, we will always refer to the GMT time zone (London) so that you can use it in any time zone you are in, but you must ensure that you regulate your operations according to the GMT time.

Sessions and times

As we have seen, Forex is a round-the-clock market and we can distinguish the various trading days thanks to the day separators. However, the trading day consists of several sessions: the European session, the American session and the Asian session, also known as London, New York and the sessions in Tokyo or Sydney.

For those who trade on Forex and specifically work on intraday, it is therefore essential to know the times at which currency exchanges take place on various markets and especially the times at which multiple sessions are open simultaneously.

I have summarized the start and end times of the main trading sessions in the London GMT time zone in the following diagram.

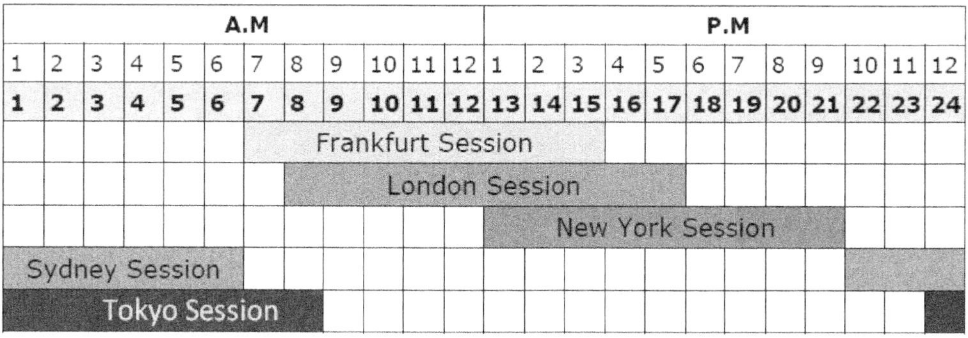

Figure 6.1

We can then divide the day into three independent operating sessions of eight hours each and understand each of their characteristics.

ASIAN SESSION:

The Asian session starts at 22:00 GMT, the time that Sydney opens. Since only Sydney is open at this time, the volumes that are traded are low and the price movements are minimal compared to other sessions.

At 00:00 GMT, Tokyo opens and the trading volume increases. Australia and Japan are relatively small markets compared to Europe and the United States and price movements are still moderate.

Spreads on major pairs are wider during these periods and liquidity is not as high as in the European and US sessions.
During the Asian session, the Australian dollar, the New Zealand dollar and the Japanese yen are the most traded currencies, because they are the national currencies of the major open markets at that time.

The most traded currency pairs during this session are:

AUD/USD	**JPY/USD**	**NZD/JPY**
AUD/JPY		**NZD/USD**
AUD/NZD		

EUROPEAN SESSION:

For Europe, the session starts at 07:00 GMT with the opening of Frankfurt, but the main speculative opportunities start at 08:00 GMT with the opening of the London session, while Tokyo is in the last hour of trading.

At this time, a large number of traders are participating in the market; this results in larger price movements than in the Asian session, which often also prove to be of great impact on the sentiments of the day.

During the European session there are no currency pairs that behave differently than usual, so, in general, all pairs can be traded. It is also substantially the highest volume traded in this session and as a result, spreads tend to be lower.

During the London session there is also more liquidity than any other session, with almost 38% of the total volume traded, more than New York (17%) and Japan (6%) combined.

We can therefore say that the opening moments of London are a good starting point to trade in a highly liquid market as well as finding the best opportunities.

AMERICAN SESSION:

The New York session opens at 13:00* GMT and overlaps with the London session. The trading of volumes and volatility further increases.

Even during the American session liquidity is high and spreads are low, so there are no particular currency pairs that should not be traded.

Although New York is second in London in terms of volumes, trading hastily slows down at 17:00 GMT when the London session comes to an end: volumes decrease, spreads widen again and price movements tend to stabilize. It is therefore advisable to look for trading opportunities only in the morning hours of the American session, because in the afternoon hours the prices become rather static.

*The American session (Wall Street) opens at 14:30 GMT, however <u>The Price in Time</u> strategy also takes into account the pre-market time slot from 13:00 to 14:30.

Price dynamics

To summarize what has been said in the previous Chapters, we have introduced the day separators to distinguish the trading days and we have seen how they include distinct trading sessions characterized by specific times and peculiarities.

The notions described so far on the charts can be seen below:

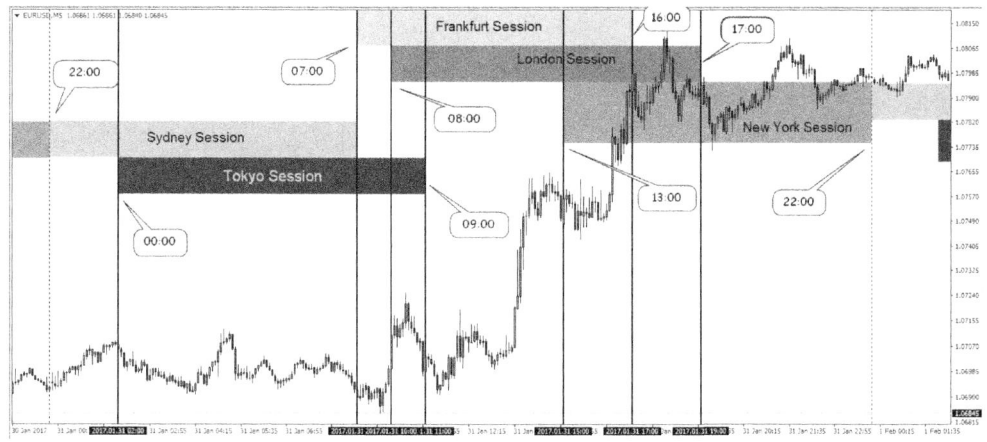

Figure 7 *EUR/USD 2017/01/31*

Figure 7 shows EUR/USD on a trading day divided into its sessions.

From this chart we can already get some very important information, but first let's further simplify the chart and split the day in just three phases - Asia, Europe and America - while adding the support of exchange volumes.

Let's see what the chart gives us:

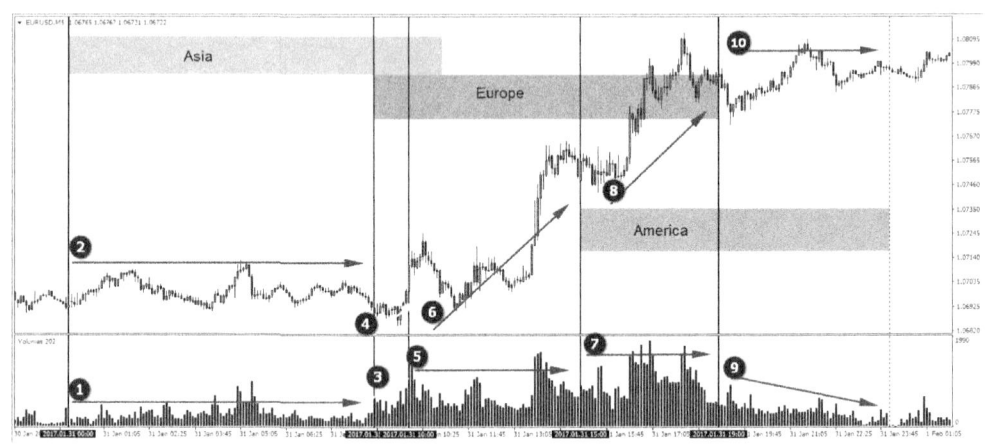

Figure 8 EUR/USD 2017/01/31

As you can see in Figure 8, the price dynamics are immediately noticeable:

1) In Asia, the volumes traded are low
2) Price movements are minimal compared to other sessions
3) Frankfurt opens, volumes begin to increase
4) Price movements are becoming more frantic
5) London opens, volumes further increase
6) Large price movements, the market becomes directional
7) New York opens overlapping with London, volumes at the peak for the day
8) Prices maintain directionality (or invert)
9) London closes, volumes decrease
10) The prices tend to stabilize, they become static

Although each session is unique, their interaction creates price dynamics that generally occur every day, creating trading opportunities that can be exploited. So we know that during the Asian session the market is quite lateral, so there are not many opportunities to capture large movements.

On the contrary, with the opening of Europe - Frankfurt before and London an hour later - the movements that are generated often create the trend of the day giving us the opportunity to take advantage and capture part of it.

It must be said, however, that the trend of the day generated by London does not always remain that way. At the opening of New York, in fact, with the arrival of America, the high volume of trade achieved combined with the publication of important economic data gives rise to a time band (from 13:00 to 17:00 GMT) which is quite delicate, where it is not uncommon to see large reversal movements that can also reabsorb the entire movement triggered by London.

It goes without saying that even these reversals offer us the opportunity to seize another trading opportunity.

Below I will show you some examples in which you can see the recurrence of these daily dynamics:

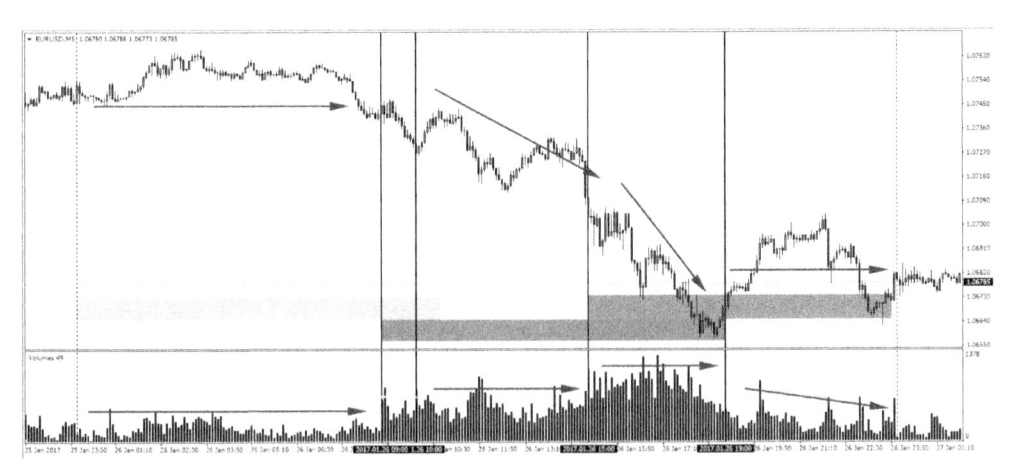

Figure 9 EUR/USD 2017/01/26

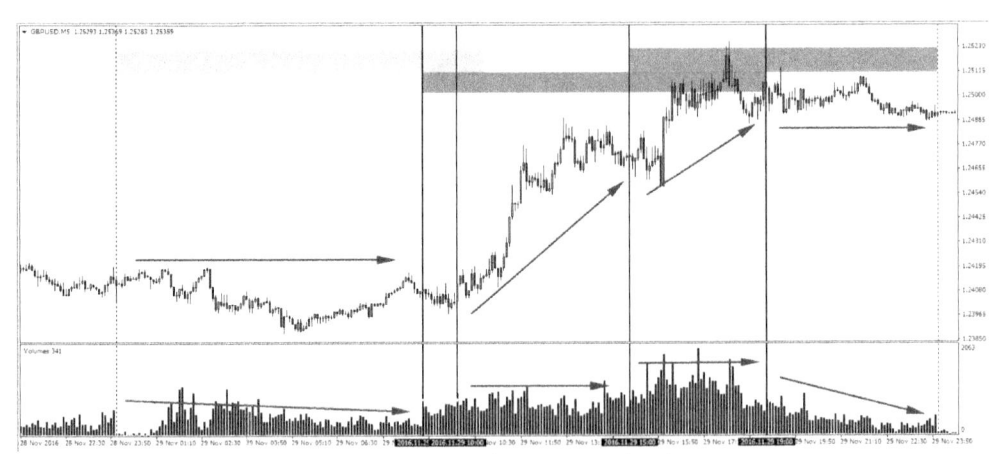

Figure 10 GBP/USD 2017/11/29

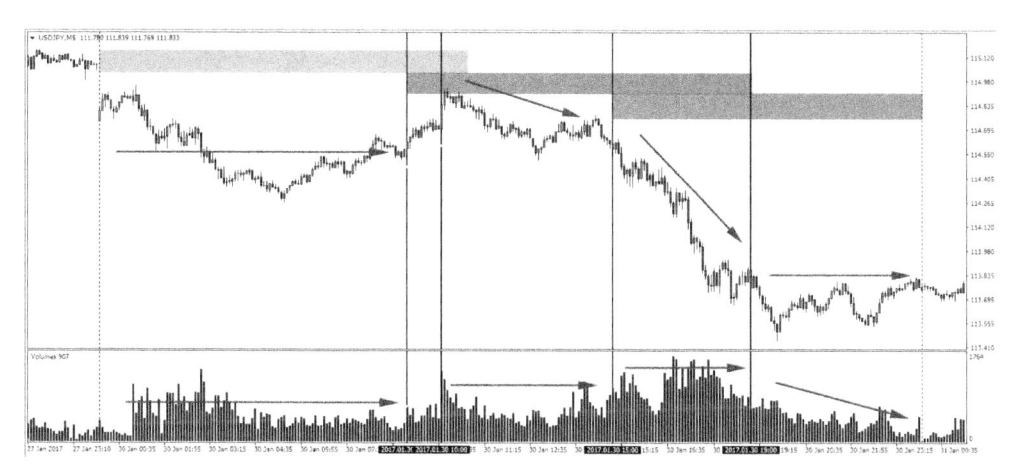

Figure 11 USD/JPY 2017/01/30

As you can see in Figures 9, 10 and 11, the price dynamics are repeated:

- Laterality with the Asian session;
- When Europe opens up, the market becomes directional;
- When America opens, the market maintains the directionality initiated by London.

Or, as I mentioned earlier, the market reverses:

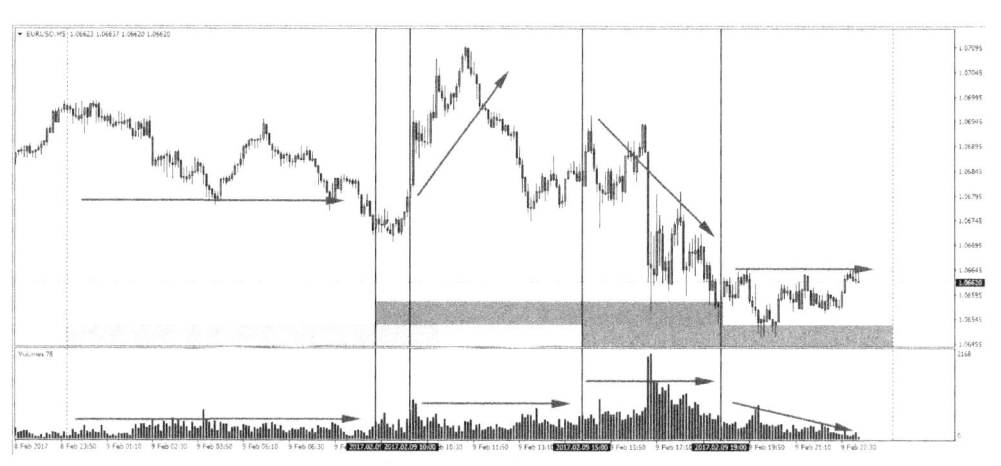

Figure 12 EUR/USD 2017/02/09

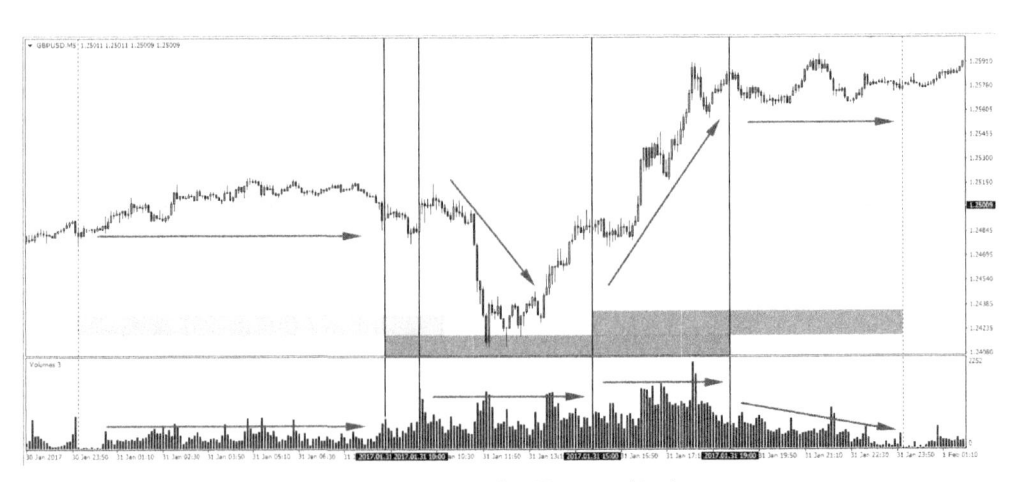

Figure 13 GBP/USD 2017/01/31

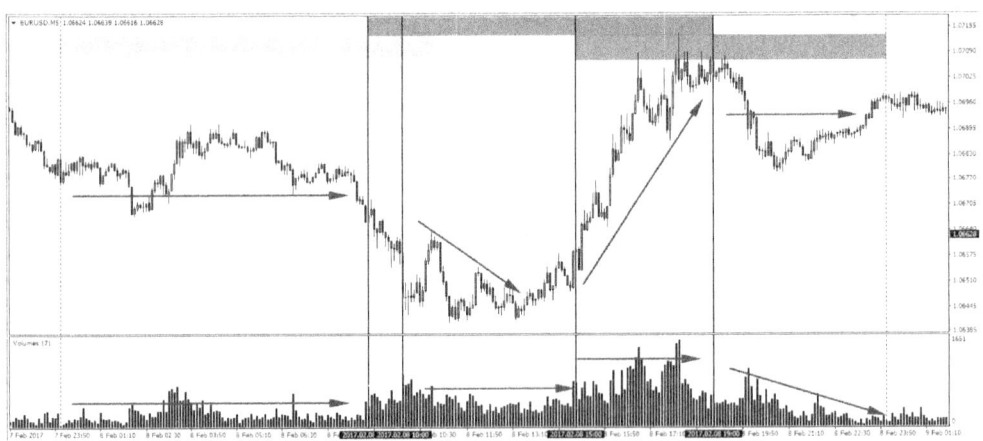

Figure 14 EUR/USD 2017/02/08

In Figures 12, 13 and 14 you can see how with the opening of New York, the trend of the day can also reverse, until it completely reabsorbs the previous movement.

Therefore, the recurrence of these dynamics tells us to:

- Exclude the Asian session
- Trade during the European session
- Trade during the American session
- Exclude the American session after 17:00 GMT (when London closes)

"Abnormal" days

Obviously, as you can imagine, the dynamics described above are not always this way, otherwise the market would be too predictable and we would have found the "Holy Grail" of trading.

However, there are days that I simply call "anomalous", because the price changes move in a different way from the usual "routine".

Let's look at the following charts:

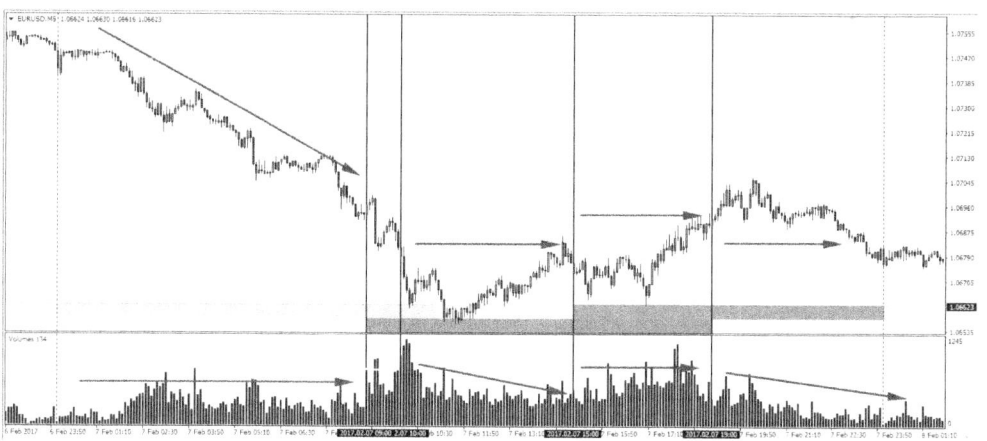

Figure 15 EUR/USD 2017/02/07

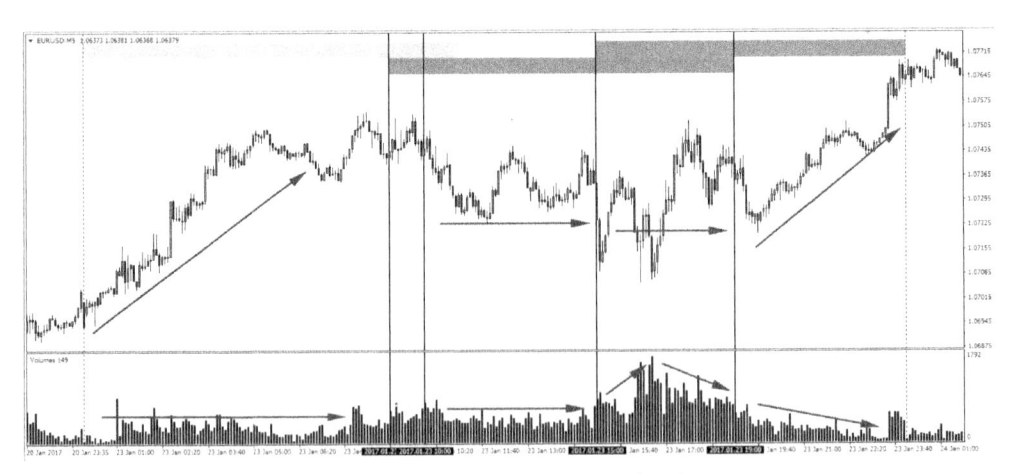

Figure 16 EUR/USD 2017/01/23

In Figures 15 and 16 you can see how, despite a normal volume behaviour, the prices at the opening of the Asian session are already starting with a strong directional movement.

Important movements during the Asian session should warn us, because it is very likely that with the opening of Europe, it will be a day of laterality and as a result we risk being trapped with our trade for the rest of the session.

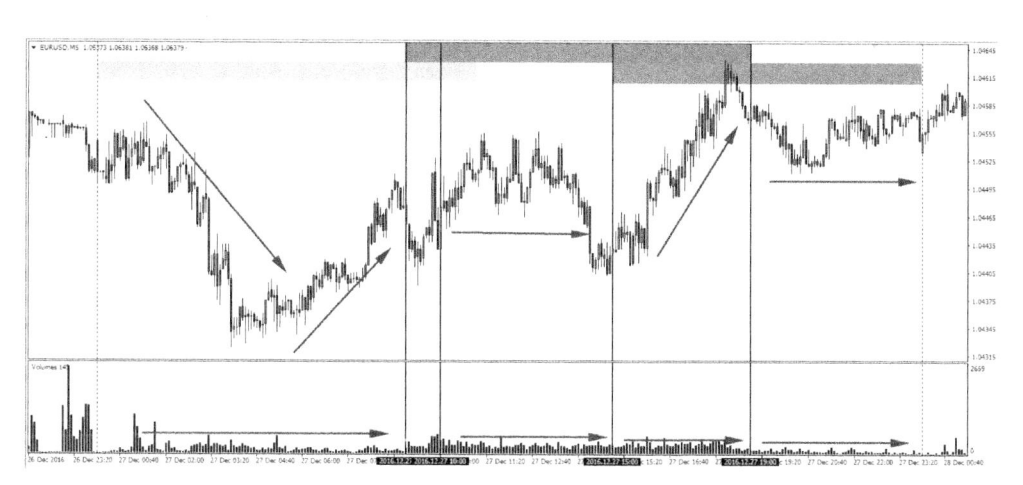

Figure 17 EUR/USD 2016/12/27

However, in Figure 17, in addition to the anomaly of the price movement in the Asian session, we also notice an anomaly of the volumes. Without looking specifically for the amount of volumes traded - which would be superfluous - at first glance we immediately notice that, compared to the norm, there is a low amount of volumes traded due to the specific day of the calendar.

As you can see, the chart is in fact the one relating to December 27: we are in the middle of the Christmas holidays and as a result, there is a low participation in the market from the big ones which goes on to compromise the "normal balance" of the daily market.

In summary, to ensure that *The Price in Time* strategy is applied effectively, we will have to exclude the days that will have exceptional characteristics in advance.

Below is a short list:

- Strong price movement in the Asian session
- Waiting for important macroeconomic data (Nonfarm Payrolls, FED and ECB speeches)
- Political news of major importance
- Catastrophes (natural events, attacks, wars)
- National holidays
- Public holidays

On the net you can easily find the calendars of the various national public holidays of the main world stock exchanges. I would recommend that you check them and refrain from trading (at least with our method) when even one of them is closed. There are days during the year when the Forex market is still open, but New York or London are closed for holidays.

Well, these factors - as we have seen - influence the normal interaction between a session and the other thus causing abnormal price behavior that would put our operations at risk.

Let me give you an example:

On the fourth Thursday of November (*Thanksgiving Day*) or the fourth of July (*Independence Day*), the American stock exchange is closed, but the Asia and Europe stock exchanges remain open. Nevertheless, the market tends to be static and does not allow for the price movements we are looking for.

In the chart in Figure 18 we can see how because of the *Presidents' Day* on Monday,

February 20, 2017, Wall Street was closed for national public holidays and although the European stock exchanges were opened regularly, the market remained in a laterality phase throughout the day.

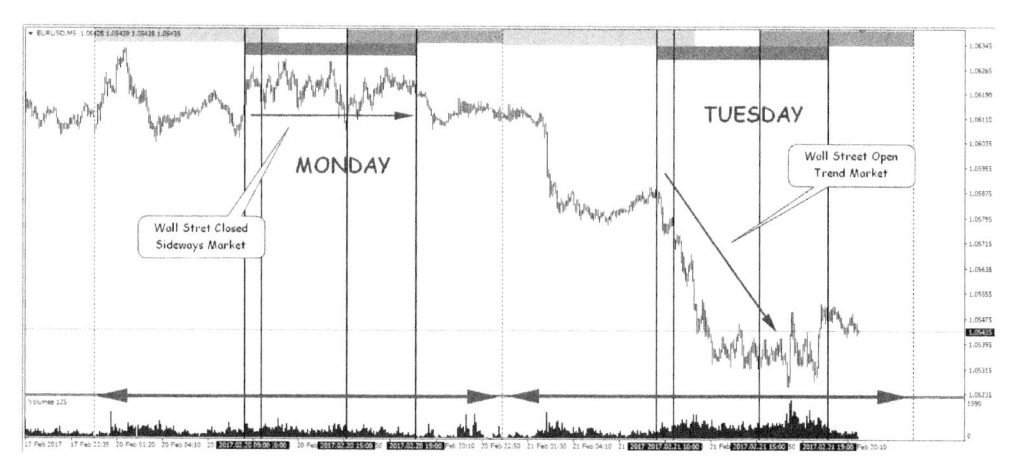

Figure 18 EUR/USD 2017/02/20 - 2017/02/21

The following day, however, with the reopening of Wall Street, the market regained its usual dynamics giving rise to an already important trend with the opening of Frankfurt (European session).

The importance of the opening price

As you have seen in the previous charts (from Figure 8 to Figure 14), excluding the Asian session - during which the market remains mainly in the lateral phase - at the opening of the European session there are large price movements that often result in important intraday trends.

Well, the first factor to take into account in order to take advantage of these movements is the opening price of the European session.

The opening price is the point from which all daily activity originates; it is a very important price level according to which big traders move from a *long* vision to a *short* vision (and vice versa). We can therefore consider the opening as the crossing point representing the sentiment of the day: if the price passes above the opening level we will go *long*; vice versa, if the price passes below the opening level, we will go *short*.

Let's look at what the charts have to say:

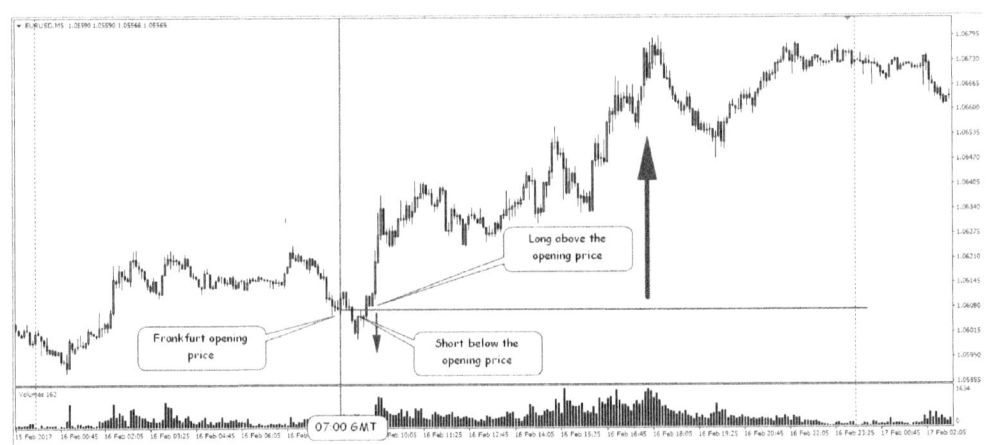

Figure 19 EUR/USD 2017/02/16.

In Figure 19 we can see the market falling below the opening price represented by the blue line and then immediately changing direction and starting upwards with a strong trend.

Hypothetically, if we had entered *short* at the break of the blue line and placed a small stop loss just above it, the trade would have stopped because the market would not have allowed us enough movement to look for a profit.

Then, we would return with a *long* trade at the upward break of the blue line and - as you can see - the market would give us the opportunity to go and capture a big profit and also recover the stop loss of the previous trade.

Let's look at some more examples:

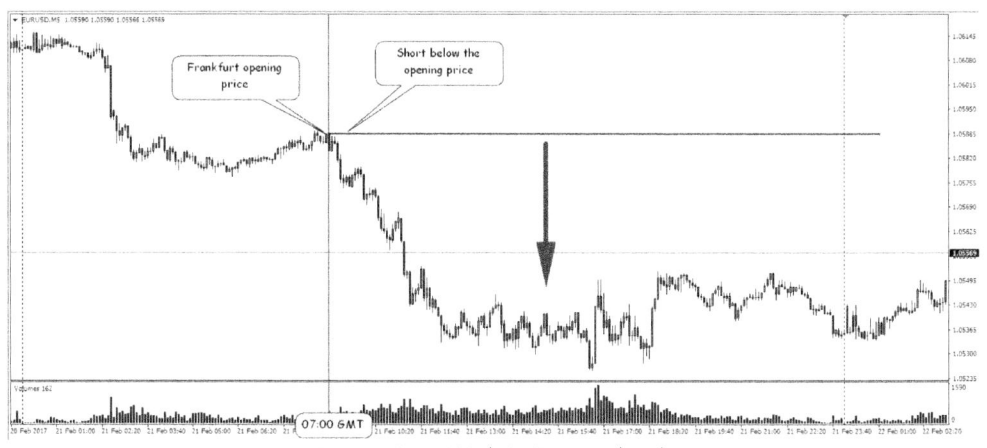

Figure 20 EUR/USD 2017/02/21

Figure 20 shows us a day that is far too easy to trade: it opens Europe with Frankfurt and the market starts immediately with a strong downward trend; a hypothetical *short* under the blue line would have allowed us to capture a nice profit here too.

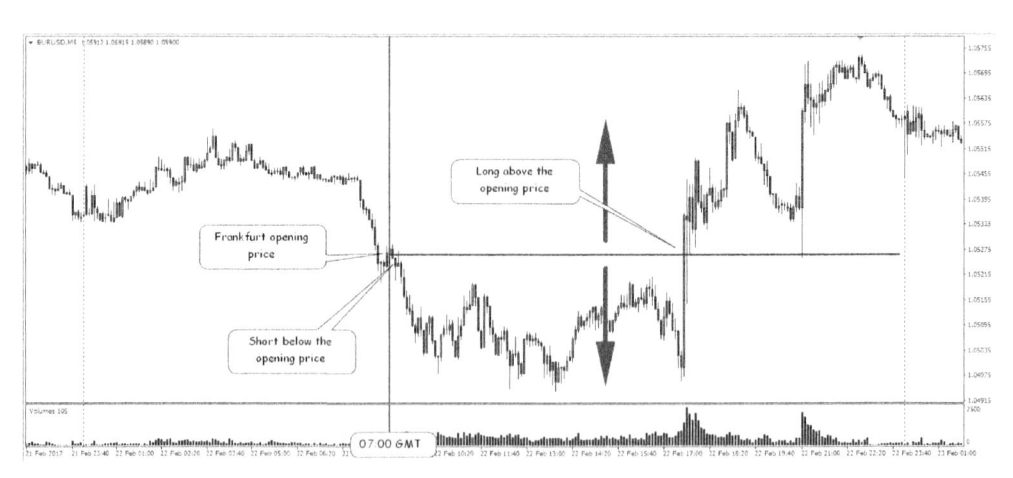

Figure 21 EUR/USD 2017/02/22

Figure 21 shows a more balanced day between buyers and sellers, so *short* under the opening with a good chance of making a profit; then we can see how, after the opening of New York (13:00 GMT), during the American session the market has completely reversed direction going on to reabsorb the movement made by London and then breaking the blue line upwards. In this case, too, a *long* entry would have given us a further increase in profit.

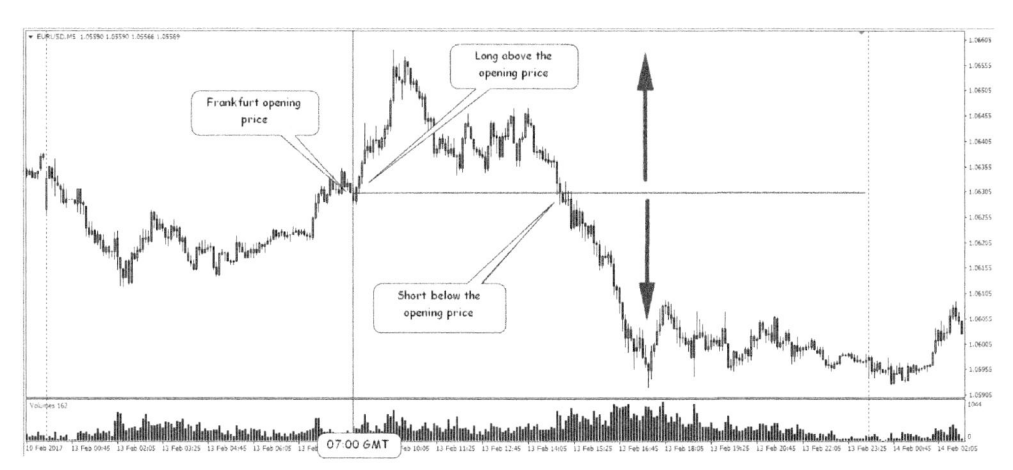

Figure 22 EUR/USD 2017/02/13

Figure 22 shows another instance of *long* at the opening of Frankfurt, a market that reverses during the American session and *short* at the break-down of the blue line. Once again on this day there are two profit opportunities, first *long* and then *short*.

We can therefore see how, through the opening price, it is possible to determine operational indications. Entering *long* and *short*, only when we pass above or below that level, however, would still lead to an unprofitable trading, because without specific operating rules that indicate exactly when to enter and exit our trades we would be nothing more than traders at a loss and the market would have the better of us.

However, we have an element of fundamental importance from which to start to create the basis of a solid structure for our strategy.

Determining the NTZ area

An important feature of the European session is certainly what I call the double opening, namely the opening of Frankfurt at 07:00 and the opening of London at 08:00. At this time there is an increase in volumes, but it is still not enough to generate real trends; as a result, most of the time the market moves frantically but still remains within a range limited to a few pips.

Well, the price distance that is formed between the minimum and the maximum in this temporal band determines the range that goes to form our "NO TRADING ZONE" (NTZ), that is an area within which you never have to enter to market for the rest of the trading day. In continuation we will see why.

The following chart represents a description of what I said: green indicates the time band that goes from 07:00 (opening of Frankfurt) to 08:00 (opening of London), while the red dashed lines respectively represent the minimum and the maximum of price formed within this hour, thus determining the NTZ area.

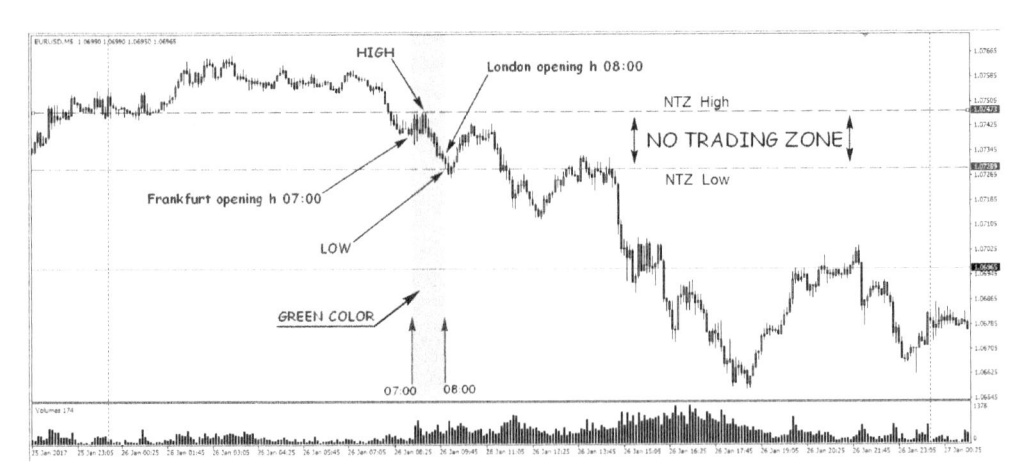

Figure 23 *EUR/USD 2017/01/26*

Basically, since the opening level in Frankfurt, it is the market itself that tells us what the first relevant support is (which we will call NTZ LOW) and what the first relevant resistance is (which we will call NTZ HIGH) that the market meets until the opening in London. NTZ HIGH and NTZ LOW are two very important levels because, starting from a price of equilibrium between buyers and sellers determined by the end of the negotiations of the Asian session, they are respectively the first support and the first resistance beyond which the still weak market is unable to reach. This means that these two price levels are particularly "felt" by institutions throughout the trading day.

Taking a step back, hence, the reason why we should not trade within the NTZ is because of the correspondence between the opening of the European session and the end of the negotiations of the Asian session, whereby the struggle between buyers and sellers has come to an end and the price is perceived by the market as "right price". The area that is formed with the first support and resistance around it, as we have just seen goes to determine a range for which, if the price goes above it creates an imbalance that triggers a force from the buyers (and traders can see a signal to buy) and vice versa, if the price goes below, the strength of the sellers is triggered (and traders can see a signal to sell). If the price is inside the NTZ, since there is no imbalance between buyers and sellers, the market does not take directionality and you can not know which direction to expect (either *long* or *short*).

This concept remains valid throughout the trading day and occurs every time the price returns into the NTZ area and until 22:00, when New York closes, since the NTZ is a highly sensitive price area for institutional investors.

Entry point

As we have seen, the NTZ area - which always has the opening of the European session within it - acts as a watershed between buyers and sellers creating a neutral price zone. Having said that, it is easy to see that when it breaks upwards we will have a *long* entry signal, while when it breaks downwards we will have a *short* entry signal.

Our entry signal is triggered <u>after 08:00</u> (opening of London), <u>when the price breaks upwards or downwards in the NTZ area</u>. Since the NTZ breakout can occur at any time (i.e. the price can break the NTZ in the *long* or *short* direction immediately after ten minutes but also after several hours) and it is not possible to know what the market will do, so as to avoid the risk of remaining in front of the monitor for hours with the finger ready to click on the *buy or sell* to wait for the breakout to happen, the strategy foresees the insertion of two pending orders of type "stop" on both sides of the NTZ, that will have to be promptly inserted just before the opening of London (two or three minutes before are enough), when by now the NTZ range has been formed.

So, in summary, we place <u>a *Buy Stop* order 1 pip above the NTZ HIGH</u> and <u>a *Sell Stop* order 1 pip below the NTZ LOW</u> just before London opens; once the breakout has taken place in the *long* or *short* direction, we will have to focus on managing the trade.

As for the second order, the one that is not executed on the other side of the NTZ, it will also have its own management modes, but we will see this later on.
For now, let's focus on the order that enters the market and the movement that is derived

from it.

In Figure 24 an example of a *long* entry:

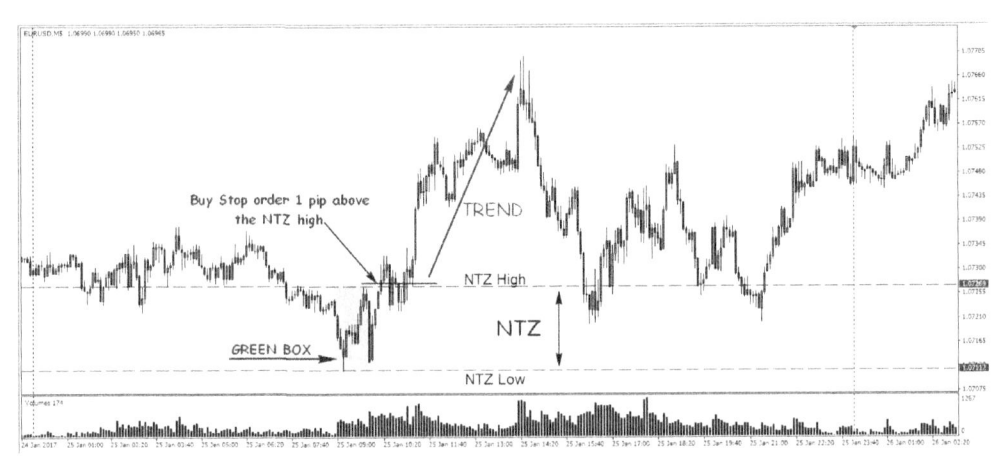

Figure 24 EUR/USD 2017/01/25

Figure 25 shows an example of a *short* entry:

Figure 25 EUR/USD 2017/01/03

Where to place Stop Loss and why

The stop loss, <u>which is always to be inserted in the platform</u> must be positioned on the opposite side of the NTZ with respect to market entry, therefore:

- Long entry, stop loss 1 pip below NTZ Low
- Short entry, stop loss 1 pip above NTZ High

Figures 24.1 and 25.1 below show the correct insertion of the stop loss.

In the case of *long* entry, the stop loss is placed 1 pip below the NTZ:

***Figure 24.1** EUR/USD 2017/01/25*

In the case of a *short* entry, the stop loss is placed 1 pip above the NTZ:

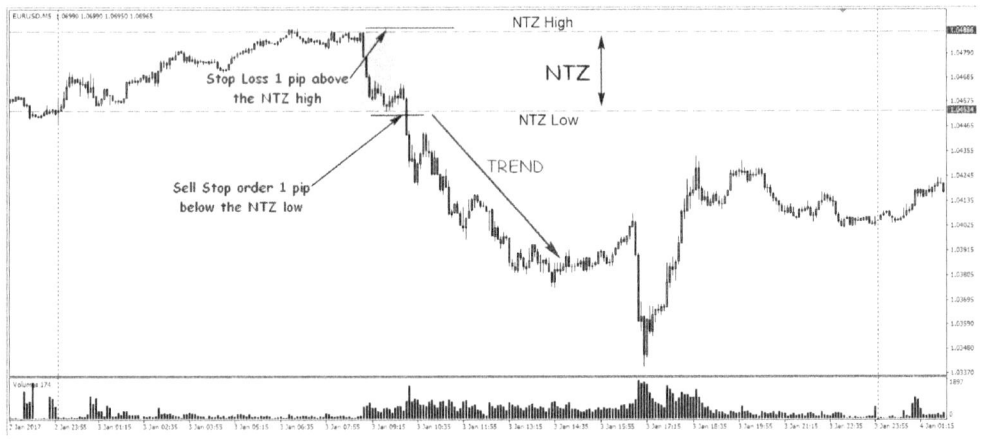

Figure 25.1 EUR/USD 2017/01/03

The stop loss is positioned in this way because, once entered to market for example in *short* direction, if in the course of the session the price goes back and overcomes the NTZ breaking it upwards, remaining inside the trade will no longer be sensible because - as previously said - the vision of the institutions (those who move the markets) passes from *short* to *long* and with a high probability that the trend of the day will change developing upwards. At this point it is clear that it no longer makes sense to insist on remaining in the market moving in a bearish direction.

Of course, the argument is made on a speculative basis if it's *long* Entry.

Take Profit levels

Once you have entered the market and placed our stop loss, you must proceed to identify what will be the future price levels on which we will place our take profits.

Well, to define these levels the best thing to do is to <u>measure the extent of the NTZ area</u> and project it from the breakout of the NTZ High for the *long* target levels and from the breakout of the NTZ Low for the *short* target levels.

Figure 26 shows how the first target level is determined in case of a *long* entry:

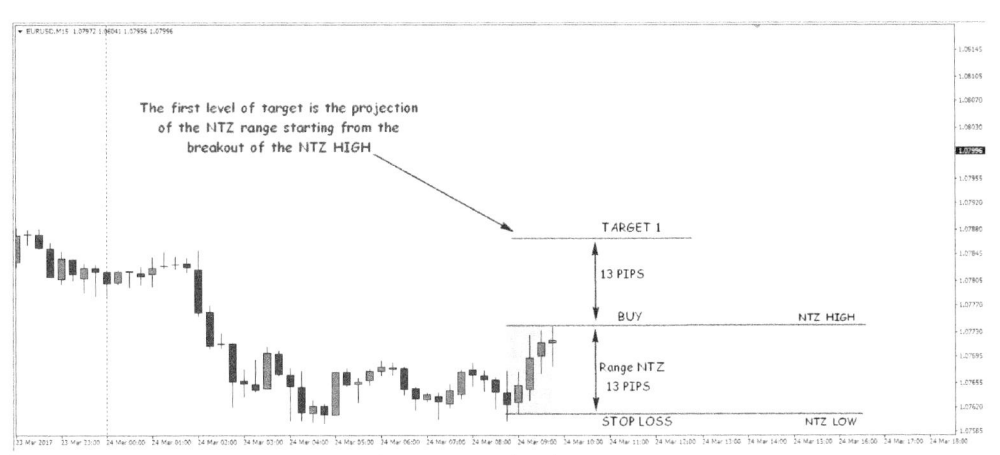

Figure 26 EUR/USD 2017/03/24

The NTZ range is nothing more than a measure of volatility at a time when Europe has opened but not all the main players in the market are active (in fact, the opening of London is pending), so we are in a phase in which the volumes begin to increase, but are not yet at the peak of trade. Consequently, the expectation is that with the opening of London volatility will increase and once the market directionality is developed, the price will move with an extension equal to or greater than the volatility taken as a reference between 07:00 and 08:00am.

We have therefore seen how, through the simple projection of the NTZ range, it is possible to determine the first level on which to go to position the first target. Now, how to determine the next levels?

Nothing could be simpler! To determine the next target levels the procedure is identical to the previous one: all you have to do is <u>project the NTZ range from the previous target level</u>. So:

- Target 2 will be obtained by projecting the NTZ range from Target 1.
- Target 3 will be obtained by projecting the NTZ range from Target 2.
- Target 4 will be obtained by projecting the NTZ range from Target 3.

and so on for subsequent targets.

In the following illustration we notice how the extension of the NTZ range projected by the target 1 determines target 2:

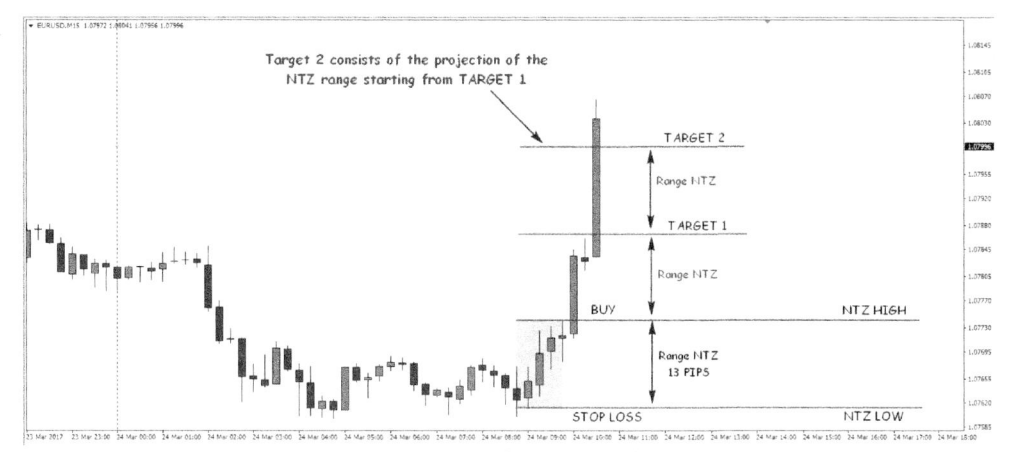

Figure 27 EUR/USD 2017/03/24

Always with the same logic, with the extension of the NTZ range from target 2 we will determine target 3:

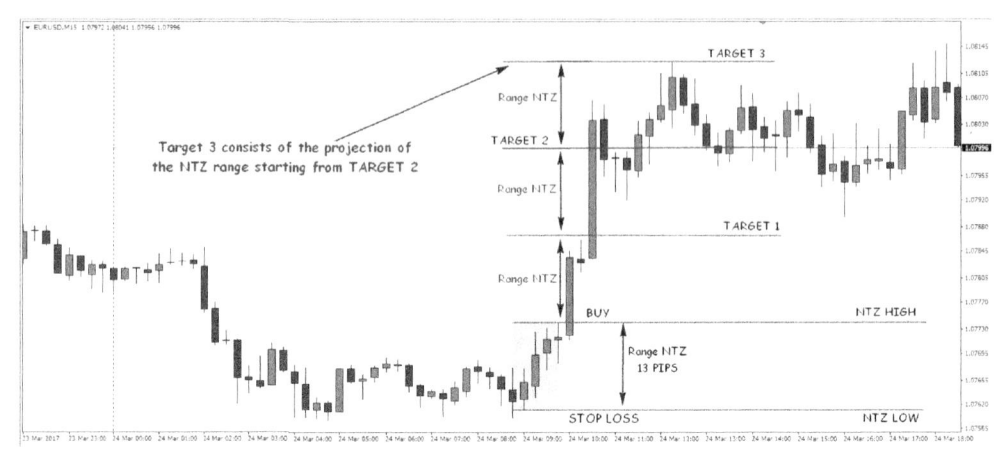

Figure 28 EUR/USD 2017/03/24

Figure 29 shows an example of a *short* in which we see EUR/USD moving up to target 4:

Figure 29 EUR/USD 2017/01/26

Supports and Resistances

Now that you know the right way to determine the take profit levels, it is important that you are aware that you will not have to calculate them as the market moves in your direction, but you will have to go and plot them immediately on the chart as soon as the NTZ range has been formed.

You should know that these price levels that you will add to the chart at the beginning of the session, in addition to being the ones on which we will place our take profits, they will also be the levels of future support and resistance.

You will notice how these levels will be used by institutions during the trading day as real supports and resistances.

Are you wondering how it is possible that the levels given by the NTZ range extension also work as supports and resistances?

It is understandable! We have always been told that you have to look back to the past to track supports and resistances, we have to scroll to the left of the chart and look for those "sensitive" price levels where the market has bounced several times causing an investor reaction.

In the following charts I have traced upwards and downwards levels of take profit: it is evident how the price reacts when it approaches them.

Figure 29.1 GBP/USD 2017/01/26

Figure 29.2 USD/JPY 2017/01/26

Figure 29.3 AUD/USD 2017/12/19

Figure 29.4 EUR/USD 2017/12/20

Really unbelievable!

Have you noticed how the market "experiences" these levels? The price bounces several times, reverses, breaks and retests them. I would say that they work precisely as supports and resistances.

That's why I think it's important to go and position our take profits at those levels (or better still, half a pip first so as not to risk seeing the price approach our take profits and then go back).

This is a minor important expedient that I wanted to reveal because I strongly believe that knowing in advance what the supports and resistances of the day to come will certainly be a great advantage over the market and indeed, even compared to other traders. I, for example, take advantage of these levels also for my scalping strategy and it is surprising to see how effective they are every time, but this is a completely different subject.

Fibonacci tips

To increase the practicality of what has been said, it is possible to predetermine the levels of *long* and *short* targets in a simple and fast way, using the tool to trace the levels of *Fibonacci* that the platform makes available to us.

Usually, when we trace the levels of *Fibonacci* (Figure 30) we identify a price range that we want to analyze, we connect the maximum to the minimum value of it and the platform automatically calculates the levels of retracements and the levels of extension of such a range.

Level		Description
4.236	%	423.6
2.618	%	261.8
1.618	%	161.8
1	%	100.0
0.618	%	61.8
0.5	%	50.0
0.382	%	38.2
0.236	%	23.6
0.0	%	0.0

Figure 30 *Preset Fibonacci levels on the platform*

In Figure 31 we see how the levels on the chart calculated according to the *Fibonacci* sequence are presented:

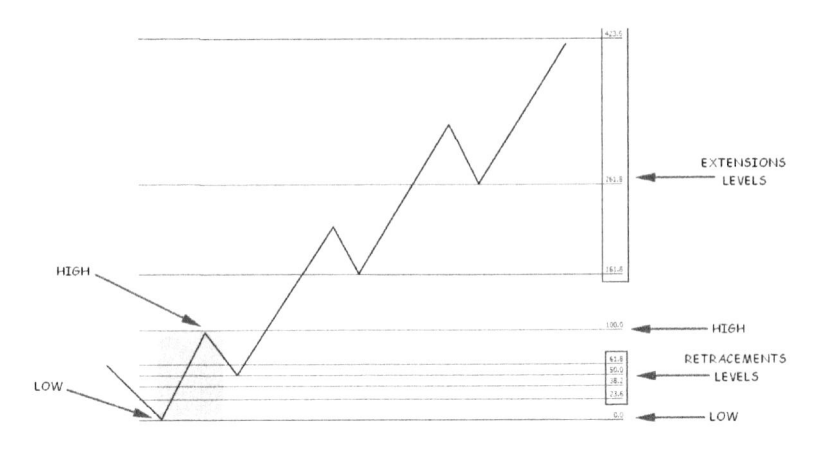

Figure 31

What we're going to do is:

1) Delete the retracement levels
2) Modify the extension levels
3) Add additional extensions below level 0.0
4) Modify the description of these levels with tags ENTRY BUY, ENTRY SELL and TP (Take profit)

The result we are going to obtain is shown in Figure 32:

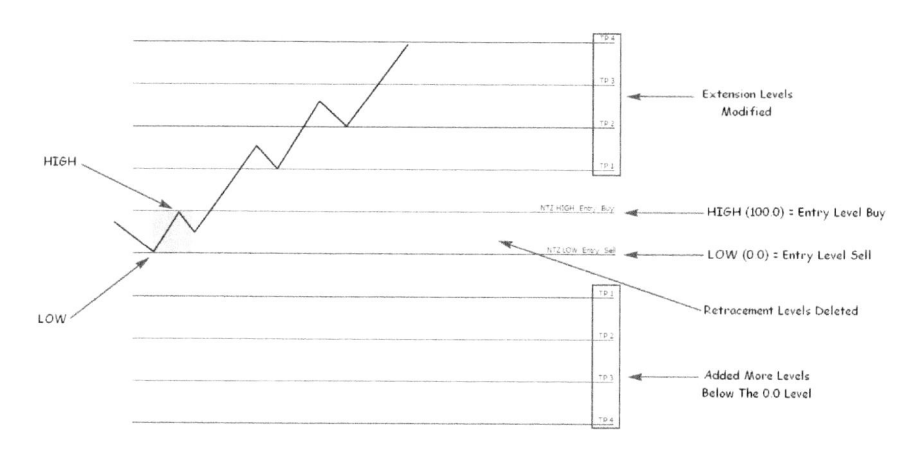

Figure 32

To achieve this, all we have to do is modify the values of the levels set by default on our platform and replace them with values equal to the amplitude of the NTZ range so that *Fibonacci* calculates the extensions of the targets both in the *long* and in the *short* directions.

In the following table (Figura 33) I have indicated, from left to right, the old levels to replace with the new ones and the old description to replace with the new one. All you have to do is enter the properties of *Fibonacci* and update the reference values.

Old Level	New Level	Old Description	New Description
0.0	Unchanged	0.0	NTZ LOW Entry Sell
0.236	Delete		
0.382	Delete		
0.5	Delete		
0.618	Delete		
1	Unchanged	100.0	NTZ HIGH Entry Buy
1.618	Change 2		TP 1
2.618	Change 3		TP 2
4.236	Change 4		TP 3
	Add 5		TP 4
	Add -1		TP 1
	Add -2		TP 2
	Add -3		TP 3
	Add -4		TP 4

Figure 33

Generally, I set my *Fibonacci* up to a maximum of four levels, but you can set to as many as you want: just add them in the settings by progressing with the sequence of the table, remember to put the negative sign for levels below 0, while for levels above 100 only the progressive number, without any sign.

Once the new values have been set, all you have to do is <u>connect the maximum to the minimum of the NTZ range</u> and *Fibonacci* will automatically calculate our take profit levels in the *long* and *short* directions.

In the following illustration we see EUR/USD at 08:00: the opening of London is the point in time when we have the minimum and maximum necessary to determine the NTZ.

Figure 34 EUR/USD 2017/04/06

Below in (Figure 35) we can see how the chart looks once the maximum is connected to the minimum with *Fibonacci*:

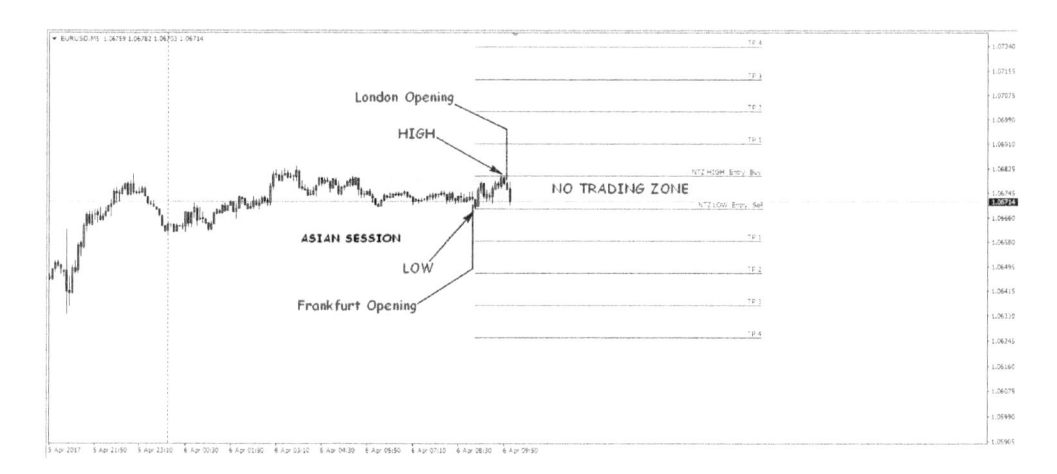

Figure 35 EUR/USD 2017/04/06

That's why we quickly determined the NTZ area and set our future take profit levels. At this point the work plan for the day is ready.

Figure 36 shows us how EUR/USD continued during the session:

Figure 36 EUR/USD 2017/04/06

NOTE:

Remember that **to connect the ends of the NTZ range you must always start from top to bottom (from maximum to minimum)** because on the contrary, you will have the reverse descriptions: "NTZ HIGH Entry Buy" at the bottom and "NTZ LOW Entry Sell" at the top (see page 149).

The NTZ boxes

We saw the correct way to enter the market, where to place the stop loss and how to calculate the levels of take profit at the beginning of the day using the NTZ area. Of course, on days when the market starts with a well-defined trend - whether it's *long* or *short* - we don't have much to worry about; we just have to wait for our trade to reach the pre-established take profits. As we have seen before, however, there are days when the market completely reverses the trend and we know that often happens after 13:00 with the opening of New York, but it is not uncommon to see this type of movement even before, that is during the first hours of the London session.

Considering the multiple variations that can occur in the arc of a day of trading, in order to always try to have a clear and orderly view of our chart, I have therefore decided to subdivide the NTZ area in three colored boxes, which graphically represent the three main time slots and will have the purpose of helping us to understand with a glance at what stage of the day we are in so as to always have an idea of the type of movement that we should expect.

We then subdivide the NTZ area in this way:

GREEN BOX

The time range from 07:00 to 08:00 is used to determine the NTZ range through the minimum and maximum that are formed within it.

PEACH BOX

The time slot from 08:00 to 13:00 represents the morning session in London, a phase of trading in which large price movements develop and the market becomes directional.

TURQUOISE BOX

The time slot from 13:00 to 17:00 represents:

- at 13:00 the time when New York opens and the London afternoon session begins, the market can maintain or reverse the trend;
- at 17:00 the time when London closes and the Europe/America sessions are no longer overlapping, volumes decrease and therefore it is no longer advisable to stay on the market.

Below you will find a series of charts with the NTZ subdivided into the three boxes mentioned above, so that you can see the possible scenarios that may occur and at the same time notice the correlation between market movements and the time slot in which we find ourselves:

Figure 37 *EUR/USD 2017/12/20*

In Figure 37 we see EUR/USD breaking the NTZ High, reaching the first take profit, returning to the NTZ area and assuming directionality with the opening of the New York session by reaching take profit 2, 3 and 4. It should be noted that, after the closure of London, the market enters into laterality.

Let us now look at another possible scenario:

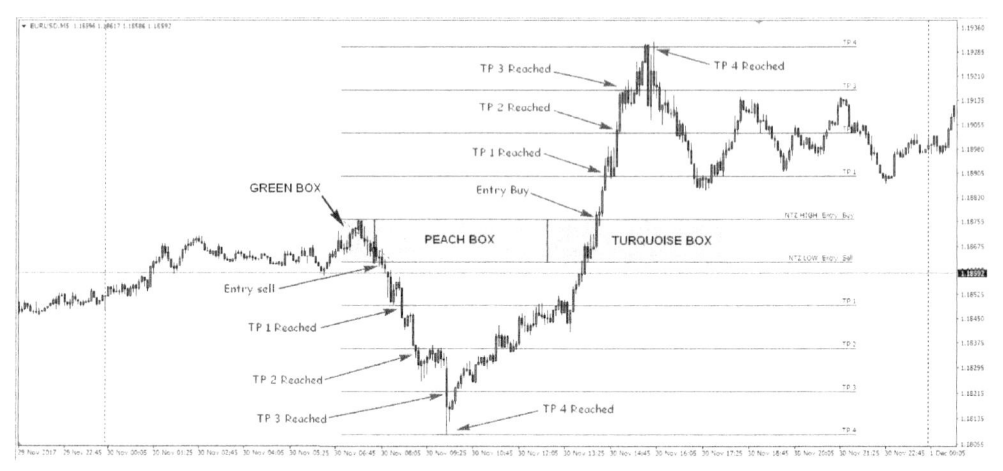

Figure 38 EUR/USD 2017/11/30

Figure 38 shows a day that is far too generous. On a pair like EUR/USD such dynamic sessions don't often happen, but it's interesting to see how at the opening of London a beautiful *short* movement started and went as far as reach take profit 4. Afterwards, we notice that during the morning in London the bearish movement was already completely reabsorbed until it reached the NTZ area and then started with a bullish trend during the American session also reaching in this case the take profit 4. Then, as usual, the closure of London and laterality followed.

Yet another scenario:

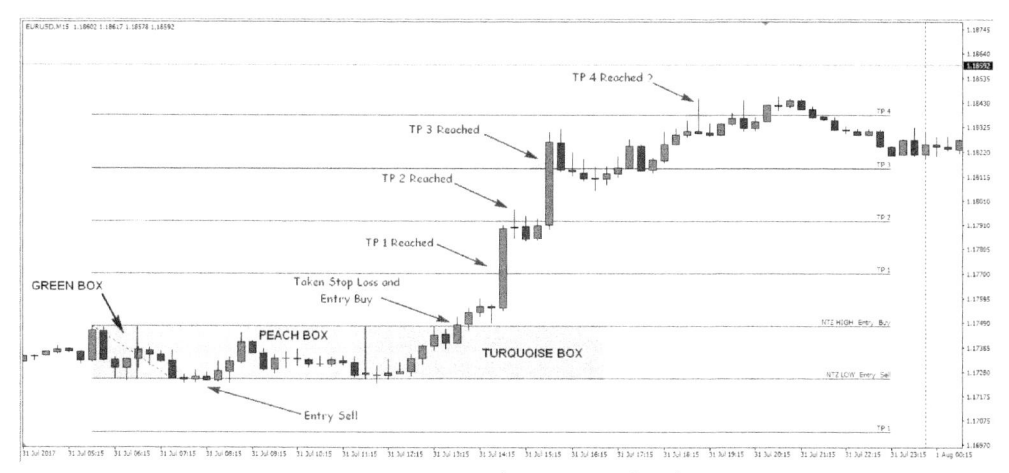

Figure 39 EUR/USD 2017/07/31

Figure 39 represents another type of day: As London opens, the market breaks down the low NTZ, our *Sell Stop* order is triggered, we find ourselves at the market and we see EUR/USD entering a phase of laterality that lasts until the afternoon. It is only after the opening of New York session that the market takes a decidedly bullish direction, thus reaching take profit 4.

On take profit 4 you can see a question mark. This has been inserted because, even if take profit 4 has actually been reached, after 17:00 (i.e. at the close of London) volumes drop dramatically and a lateral phase is expected, in these cases the trade must be closed manually to avoid remaining on the market in a phase of congestion.

Another example, this time on GBP/USD:

Figure 40 GBP/USD 2017/11/22

Figure 40 shows GBP/USD breaking down the NTZ and reaching take profit 1. Then we see how, with the opening of New York, the market decisively reverses its direction giving rise to a strong upward trend.

Afterwards, *long* entry, take profit 1 and 2 are reached by 17:00 which is the closing time in London; at this point we will also close our business day because we know that at this time we can expect a lateral phase and therefore, it would not be appropriate to go looking for further targets.

Nevertheless, we see that the trend continues even after 17:00 and reaches take profit 3 and 4. Here again there is a question mark at take 3 and 4 for the same reasons as Figure 39.

As you have seen from the examples above, there are many and varied situations that can arise every day; market movements often start, reverse or end with the beginning and end of the Europe/America sessions. I have decided to introduce the NTZ boxes to show you some of the possible scenarios, so that you can always have an idea of what movements to expect at any time of the day and deal with every situation that will arise with mastery and confidence thanks to the operating rules that we will see later combined with appropriate money management.

Remember:

The NTZ boxes are not necessary for operational purposes, because it is not only important, but also sufficient to keep in mind the London time (GMT) to know what kind of movements to expect, but, however, by drawing them on the chart at the beginning of the day can certainly offer us a valuable visual aid.

The natural cycle of ranges

In the Chapter of "abnormal days" we have evaluated a series of elements to keep in mind before considering the hypothesis of trading an instrument.

Another important factor to evaluate before starting our trades is also <u>the width of the NTZ range</u>; to do this, it is necessary to measure the distance between the minimum and maximum of the NTZ area, which must not exceed 30 pips.

So, if the pair we want to trade forms an NTZ with a range below 30 pips, "OK TRADING" and we can enter our two pending orders *BUY* and SELL. Conversely, if the pair forms an NTZ with a range greater than 30 pips, "NO TRADING", and we switch to another currency pair.

This operating rule stems from a study on the "natural cycle of the range variation" by Larry Williams, according to which there is a precise frequency in the activity of the price ranges. In fact, Larry Williams shows how, in every moment and in every market, the ranges alternate from a series of limited ranges to a series of extended ranges with a tendency for cyclicity that always repeats itself.

Without dwelling too much on the explanations, we can make it easier by indicating them as focal points:

- **Small ranges are followed by large ranges**

- **Large ranges are followed by small ranges**

In fact, it would be a mistake to think that, if there is a large price movement, it will continue; most of the time, the large price movement will decrease in a period of congestion. On the contrary, if there is a small price movement, we must instead expect a large market movement.

The charts below clearly show everything that has been said:

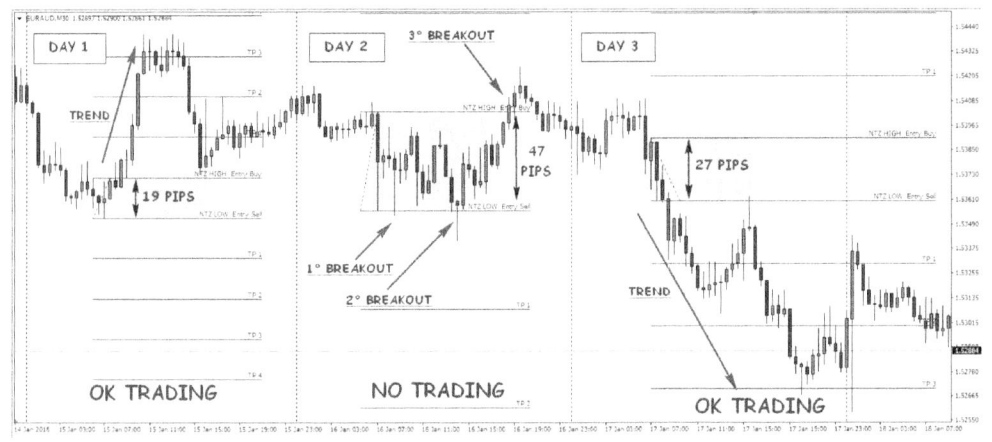

Figure 41 *EUR/AUD 2018/01/15-16-17*

Figure 41 compares three consecutive days. We can see that the first day the NTZ range has a width of 19 pips, so it is a perfect day for trading because you have a value below 30 pips and it fully respects the above parameters, therefore, if I have a small NTZ range I would expect a day with a wide range and in fact let's see how, after the *long* breakout, a trend has started that has gone up to take profit 3.

The second day instead represents a completely different situation: the market forms a NTZ range with an amplitude of 47 pips, well beyond our limit of 30 pips; so at this point we must rule out the idea of trading in advance because, after a wide range, the expectation is to see a small range (that is possibly a day of laterality), so without the possibility of going on to take those directional movements that we aspire for. In effect, although three breakouts have occurred, two on the downward side and one on the upward side, we notice the market did no take direction for the rest of the day.

On the third day the NTZ range, it measures a width of 27 pips, very close to the maximum threshold of 30 pips but still in line with our values, in this case we can operate quietly, from the small range I expect a large range and we can actually see EUR/AUD break down the NTZ low and take the desired directionality, reaching up to take profit 3.

Let's see another example:

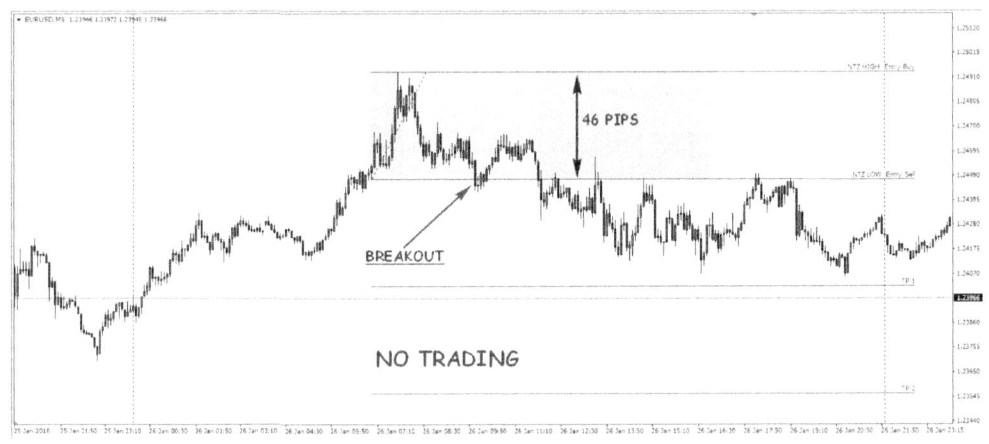

Figure 42 EUR/USD 2018/01/26

Figure 42 shows another case of the NTZ range above the preset limit (46 pips). We can see EUR/USD breaking down and remaining in a phase of laterality (highlighted in the yellow box) throughout the day, without ever reaching even the first take profit.

After analyzing most of the currency pairs and practicing this trading method for several years, I have come to the conclusion that an NTZ range between 10 and 30 pips is the most appropriate value for the correct application of the strategy. However, in addition to respecting the maximum limit, it is important to take into account the minimum limit of 10 pips. This is because, with a maximum of two trades per day (one *long* and one *short*) per currency pair scheduled through pending orders, if the NTZ range is too small, the chances are almost certain that they will be executed in a short time from both directions due to normal market volatility and not for an actual price breakout.

Below is an example with the NTZ range below 10 pips:

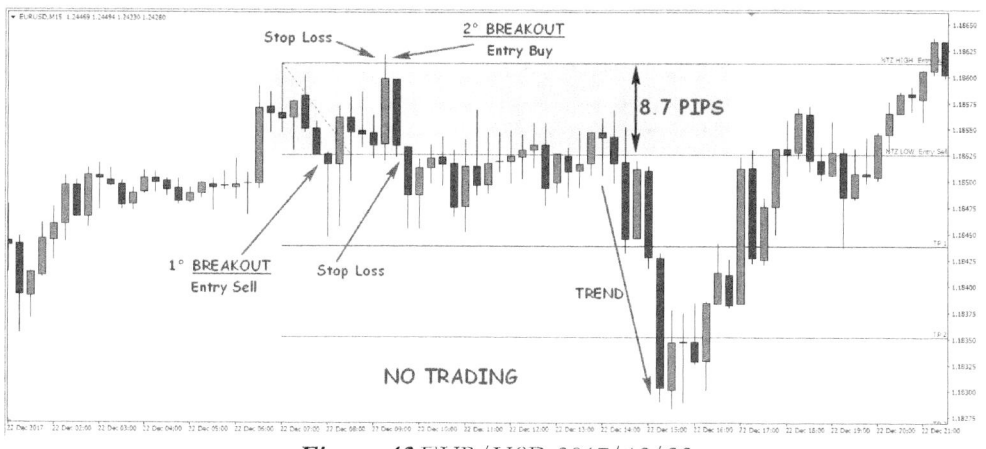

Figure 43 EUR/USD 2017/12/22

Figure 43 shows EUR/USD with an NTZ range of 8.7 pips; the value is below our minimum limit of 10 pips and is in fact too limited range to be able to place two pending orders at the end, as the average volatility (particularly after the opening of London) has a greater range than the NTZ area. In fact we can see how, before taking directionality, the market first proceeded to execute the *sell* order bringing it into stop loss and then the *buy* order, also ending in stop; all in a time span of about an hour and a half. It is probably better too avoid similar situations in advance and to save us two stop loss.

Yet another example:

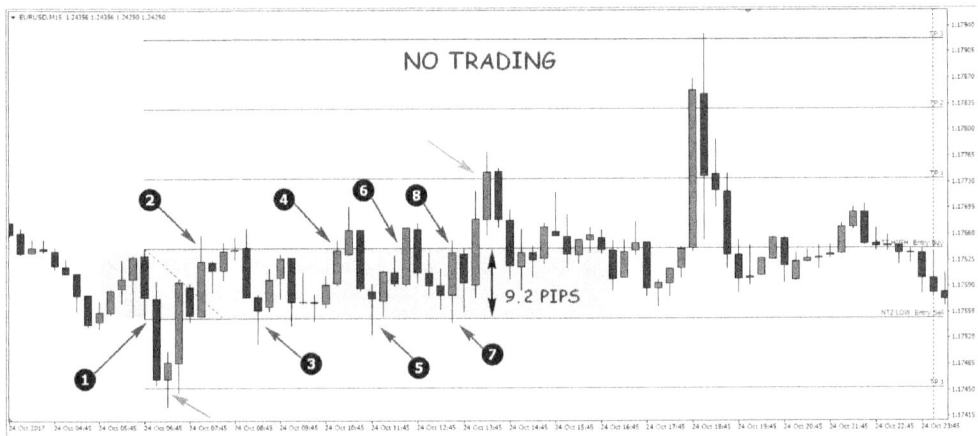

Figure 44 EUR/USD 2017/10/24

Figure 44 shows an NTZ area of 9.2 pips (again below the minimum limit of 10 pips). We can see EUR/USD reaching the first *short* take profit (orange arrow), after which we notice that, due to a static price phase, the extremities of the NTZ are invalidated several times, even with eight breakouts before the price reaches the first *long* take profit (green arrow).

The timeframe does not count

So far we have not yet talked about timeframe and yet, at this point of reading, you have already learned the basics of the strategy: you know when to enter the market, where to place the stop loss and how to determine the take profits.
"The Timeframe doesn't count!"

I know, it may seem like a strong expression but it is actually a fact: to trade intraday, with this strategy the timeframe used to look at the chart is absolutely not important, because this method is based on the price quotations that occur between 07:00 and 08:00 and this means that the price changes that occur within this time are factual data, regardless of the timeframe used to display the chart.

Let me explain. The price that is hit at the opening of Frankfurt at 07:00, the price that is hit at the opening of London at 08:00 and its maximum and minimum that are formed within this time are objective elements and can not change depending on the type of timeframe used from the type of analysis that applies or the skill of the trader. They are four elements with no interpretation or discretion and are the same for all traders in every corner of the world. That's why, every time I shared my operations in social groups and forums, I smiled when asked what timeframe I used to make those trades, because inevitably my answer was always the same: " The timeframe does not count!".

For some of them, this was a very strange answer, but how can we blame them if 90% of the people around teach us to think in terms of timeframes?

Any kind of technique that is disclosed - candlestick analysis, technical analysis figures, Elliot waves, Wolfe waves, Gann cycles, swing trading, trapping trendline divergences and breaks - needs a reference timeframe to be applied.

The fact is that markets move simultaneously in different timeframes: a trader chooses a timeframe - be it an H4, H1 or a 30 minute timeframe - and then goes looking for the entry signal. The problem is that in order to verify the authenticity of the signal itself, the trader has to analyze the market context on different timeframes, bigger and smaller and instead of getting confirmation he/she realizes that these signals, even if they come from the same market contradict each other leaving room for doubts and uncertainties.

That's why I developed *The Price in Time* method: I wanted certainties to work on. With this method I have no doubt, I'm sure, once the market hits 8:00 am I *buy* when it goes up and *sell* when it goes down with reference to objective data. End of story.

Take a look at GBP/USD in the following charts:

Figure 45 GBP/USD 2018/01/04 TF *m1*

Figure 46 GBP/USD 2018/01/04 TF *m5*

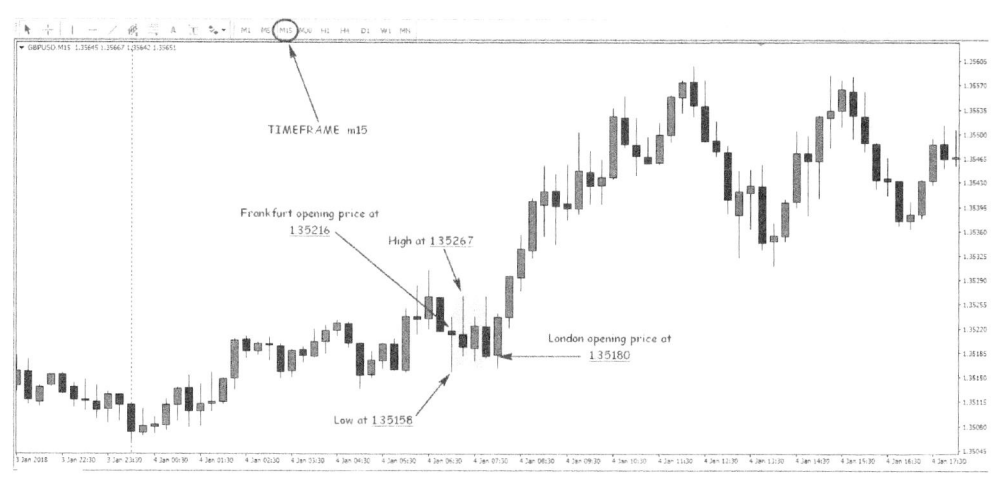

Figure 47 GBP/USD 2018/01/04 TF *m15*

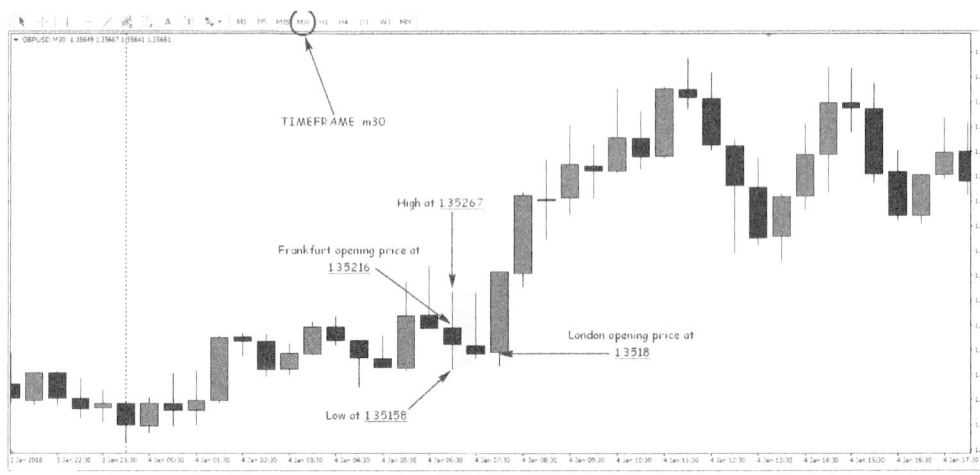

Figure 48 GBP/USD 2018/01/04 TF *m30*

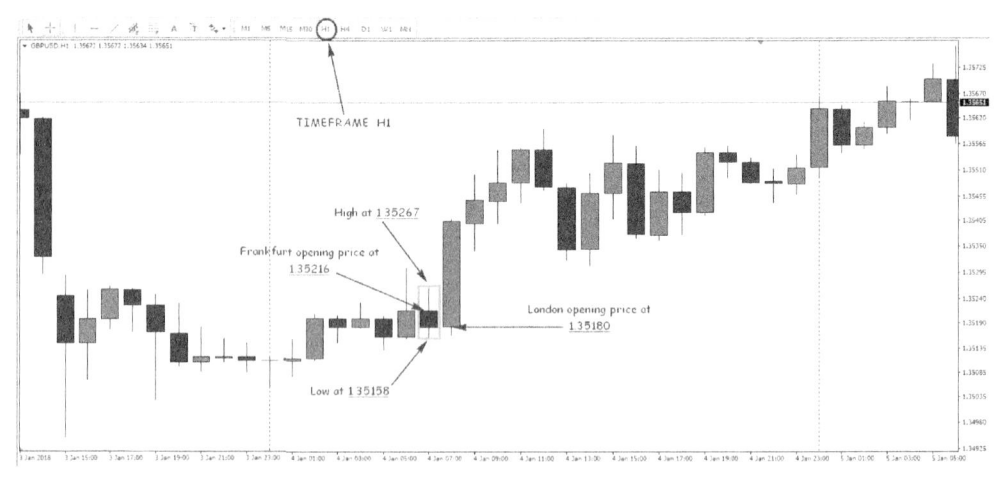

Figure 49 GBP/USD 2018/01/04 TF *h1*

As you can see, the day is the same; the timeframes change, the trend of the charts changes, but the four elements that we need to operate do not change: the four prices are hit in this time slot regardless of any doubt or uncertainty.

Of course, working on the platform with a 4-hour chart or daily would not make sense, it would make our lives difficult trying visualize our four reference prices to trace the NTZ; that said, from the hourly chart onwards you can use the timeframe you prefer.

The trading plan

At this point it is time to talk about money management and the management of our trades, but before moving on to this topic I want to show you with a practical example of the main points of the strategy to follow, so that you can easily know how to deal with a day of trading.

First of all, we have to check the economic calendar and make sure that there are currently no national holidays, making sure that all the major world stock exchanges are open and thus avoiding running into an "abnormal day".

Subsequently, it is useful to take a look at the most important economic news of the day, such as announcements on interest rates, *Non-Pharm Payroll* or speeches by central banks in which monetary policies are announced regarding the currencies we want to trade; we must exclude all those events that, in most cases, make the day start with a consistent laterality and then end with strong price fluctuations. In short, we must avoid all those situations that could destabilize normal daily trading.

After this, we can open our chart and check if the market has remained in a lateral phase and in a limited range during the Asian session:

Figure 50 EUR/USD 2018/09/20

At this point, when two or three minutes are left until 08:00 and the double European opening is about to be opened (i.e. when the maximum and minimum between 07:00 and 08:00 are now formed), we can then trace the green box and measure its range to verify if it is between 10 and 30 pips, a value that allows us to trade:

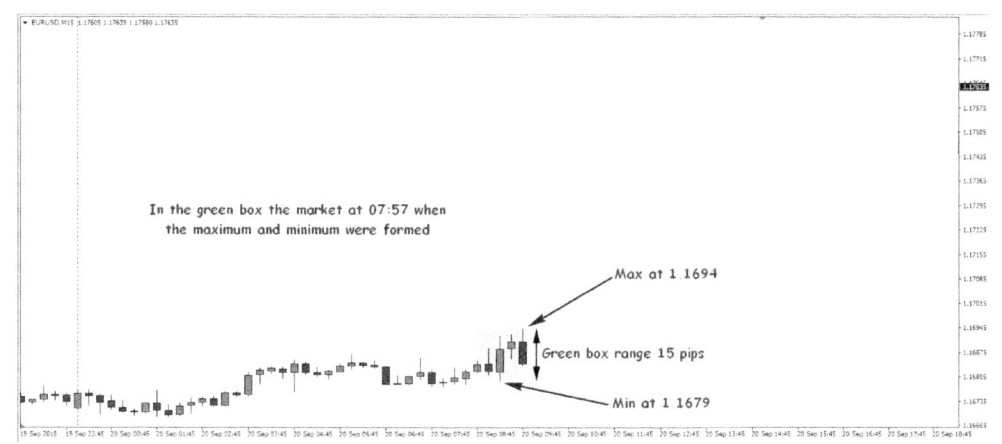

Figure 51 *EUR/USD 2018/09/20*

Now we can connect the ends of the green box with our modified *Fibonacci* (remember to always start from the maximum to the minimum) so as to determine the NTZ area with its levels of Take Profit:

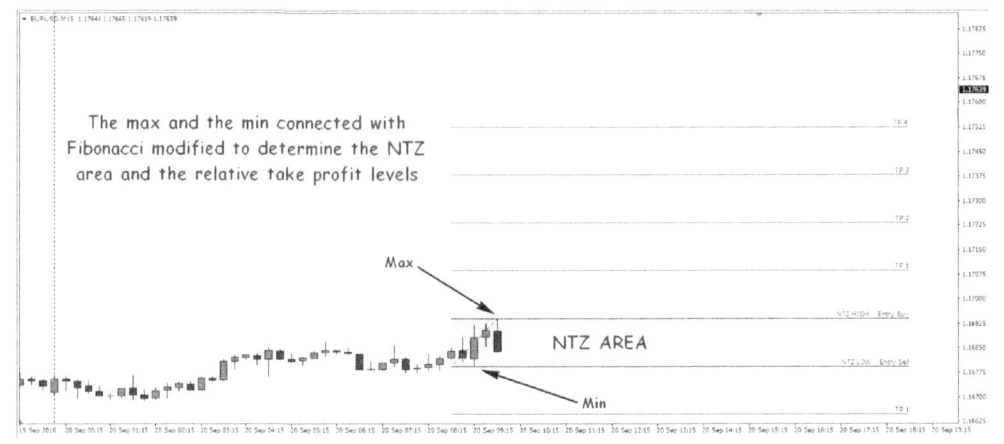

Figure 52 EUR/USD 2018/09/20

Let's now place our orders: *buy stop* 1 pip above NTZ HIGH and *sell stop* 1 pip below NTZ LOW, with the relative stop losses placed on the opposite side of the NTZ area:

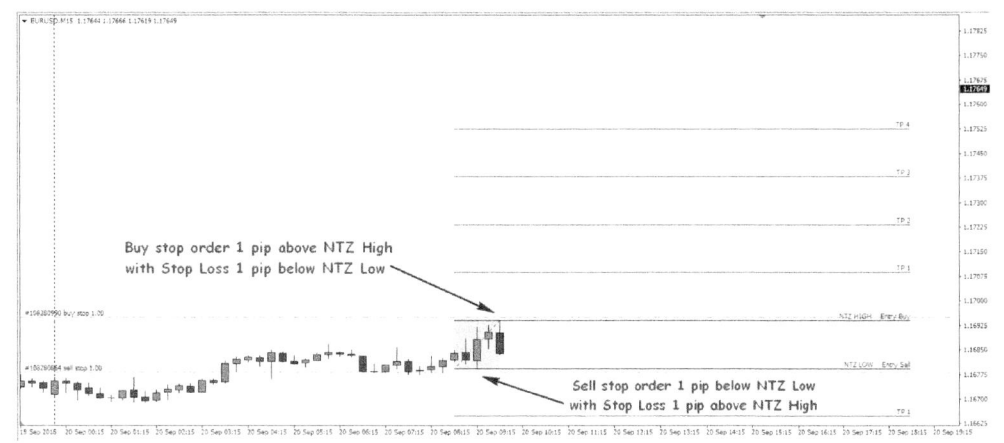

Figure 53 EUR/USD 2018/09/20

While we wait for our orders to be taken, we can confidently track the NTZ boxes to help us understand what stage of the session we are at all times:

Figure 54 EUR/USD 2018/09/20

Once the trading plan has been prepared, all we have to do is wait for the market. In the following chart (Figure 55) we see the breakout upwards with a nice directional movement that even went beyond take profit 4 and the *sell stop* order that was canceled:

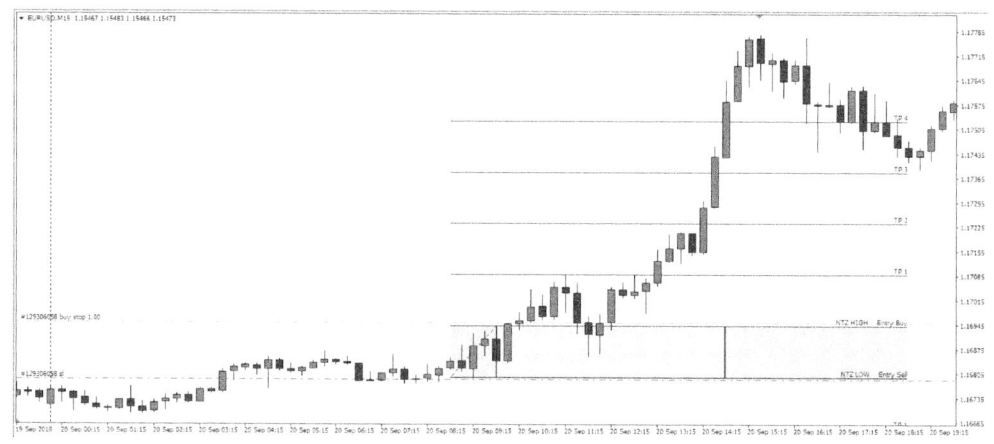

Figure 55 *EUR/USD 2018/09/20*

These are basically the steps you need to take to plan your trading day.

To gain the right practicality, I recommend that you start by trading with a single currency pair, once you have gained experience, you can switch to more pairs, of course without exaggerating because the simultaneous management of too many operations would become difficult. Personally, I always work with a maximum of three currency pairs, which are well selected and allow me to trade in peace with excellent satisfaction.

Later we will see how, through the models of trade management, the stop loss and the pending order that is not executed will be managed.

In the following page you will find a list that shows every step of the procedure to be performed.

CHECKLIST

- Check the economic calendar (national holidays and important news)

- Check that the Asian session was lateral (no trend)

- 2 or 3 minutes before 08:00, link the maximum to the minimum that were formed between 07:00 and 08:00 determining the NTZ and Take Profit levels

- Measure the NTZ range and make sure it's between 10 and 30 pips.

- Place your pending orders 1 pip above NTZ HIGH and 1 pip below NTZ Low

- Enter the Stop Losses of both pending orders

- Track the NTZ boxes for visual help (optional)

- Focus on trade management

Money management

Now that we have created our trading plan, including when and where to enter the market, where to place the stop loss and how to determine the take profits, it is time to talk about the most important element of trading, that in my opinion makes the difference between a successful trader and a losing trader: money management.

Money management is nothing more than a set of rules designed to first of all figure out how much capital to invest in trading and how much capital to risk per operation and to ensure proper management of trades in order to limit losses as much as possible and maximize profits.

You will decide these rules based on the capital you have available to invest, always keeping in mind the main objective of money management itself: which is to preserve your capital even in the face of a series of negative trades so that you can ensure a constant presence in the financial markets without running the risk of being swept away in a short time.

Remember that the markets are ruthless and it is a hard fight to try to beat them every day, but if you stick with discipline to your money management plan success is guaranteed!

To establish our rules we must contextualize money management in every aspect. As you probably already know, it is divided into three fundamental branches which are inseparable from each other:

- Money management

- Risk management / Position sizing

- Risk reward

Money management:

Many books and articles have been published on money management that talk about the right amount of capital to be used for each trade.
But before discussing this topic, I would like to take a little step back and talk to you about something that no one ever bothered to delve into and that in my opinion is a fundamental point that underlies everything.

How much capital am I willing to invest in trading?
How much money do I have to pay to the Broker?
How much money can I withdraw?

Thinking about it, you know that the greater the capital of the account, the higher the profits that can be generated, so logically you try to pour as much money into the account as possible.

<u>Never make that mistake!</u>

Opening a trading account and pouring all your accumulated savings acquired with so much effort with the intention of making higher profits is the most common and widespread error among retail traders.

We must never forget that, while it is true that the Forex market can generate very high profits, it is also true that it is a high-risk market and therefore we must always bear in mind that even our savings, once deposited into the account will be subjected to the same great risk, even if the strategy we use is statistically successful. Even though money management is as accurate as possible, it is good to keep this concept in mind and never invest all the money that we have available. Even the banks don't do it, so why should we do it?

Therefore, first of all it is necessary to establish the optimal percentage of the total capital (your savings) you want to dedicate to trading, which must be a percentage that would not compromise your financial stability even in the unfortunate case of a total loss of the investment. It is natural that all the percentages are at the discretion of the trader, but we will rely on the numerous statistics carried out by the world's biggest traders who recommend a percentage of 15-20% of the total amount in the account.

Therefore, the formula to be applied is this:

$$[TOTAL\ CAPITAL\ /\ 100] \times 15\text{-}20 = CAPITAL\ TO\ INVEST$$

So, if we assume we have $50.000 as total capital and want to apply a percentage of 20%, here is what we have to do:

$$50.000 \$ / 100 = 500 \times 20 = 10.000 \$$$

This would leave $40.000 of total capital (our savings) safe and $10.000 available for investment, so that if one day the stock exchanges collapse and our account is lost due to any reason independent of us (anything can happen in the financial markets), our economic stability would not be compromised and indeed, we would still have capital to invest in the future.

Once you have established the right amount for your initial deposit, it is useful to understand what proper withdrawal management can be. It is clear that, as profits accumulate, the account will grow; and if the account grows, the profits will increase in turn, which in turn make the account grow and so on, in a directly proportional manner.

Thinking from this point of view, then, it would be advisable to never withdraw so as to be able to see our money rise. But being traders and obviously wanting to enjoy the money earned, a good rule - and even the wisest - is to make periodic withdrawals in order to safeguard the profits accumulated and make them grow outside the trading account. Remember that the money you use for trading is always to be considered of being at risk and a good trader must always protect their profits, so the best advice is to make monthly withdrawals or at most quarterly.

A good compromise is certainly the monthly withdrawal (like it is a salary); the amount of money to be withdrawn is obviously subjective, because it depends on the objectives of the trader, but it is evident that if you withdraw a large part of the profits you would slow down the process of accumulation on the trading account and, as a result, the gains in the long run would be lower. Therefore, even in this case, it is necessary to find the right proportion: it is usually recommended to withdraw a percentage ranging from 40% (in case of quarterly withdrawal) to 60% (in case of monthly withdrawal) of the net profits obtained.

The percentage of the quarterly withdrawal (40%) is lower than the percentage of the monthly withdrawal (60%) because, by not withdrawing each month, the capital on the account will be greater; consequently, the profits will be higher and at the end of the quarter the amount of money withdrawn will be approximately similar to the amount of money that would have been withdrawn in the event of a monthly withdrawal.

That said, we will have to take into account the share of uncollected profits remaining in the account from then on as part of the equity available for trading, which will give us a good and well thought out way to place part of the accumulated profits safely and at the same time, part of the profits will remain to increase our trading account.

Risk management / Position sizing:

Now that we have seen how to best quantify the capital to be invested in trading, we can talk about proper risk management and what the right amount of money to be used for each individual trade is. In other words, it is about establishing the correct amount of money to be used in relation to the capital of our trading account (equity).
How much are we willing to lose for each trade?

I often hear that, to establish this figure, the trader must rely on his or her propensity to take risks...
I don't think so!

What is risk appetite? A question of character or courage?

If we were to hypothetically find ourselves in front of a brave trader with a good propensity to take risks, could he then risk 10-15-20% of the amount in the account for each trade?

No. That's not how it works; it's certainly not the risk appetite of the individual trader that ensures survival in the financial markets. With a percentage like the one in the example above, after a series of just 4 or more 5 consecutive negative trades, the equity of our account would inevitably be compromised and we would also end up in *the Club of Losing Traders*.

Survival in the financial markets is guaranteed by a risk percentage that enables us to easily overcome even a significant number of negative trades.

Several studies carried out by the biggest American traders have shown that the maximum percentage of loss in relation to capital must not exceed 2%; the optimal range of risk, in essence, must be between a minimum of 0.50% and a maximum of 2% of the equity.

Generally, I apply an overall risk across all the trades of 2% to my equity. Let me explain: if I enter the market with a single trade, I will risk 2% of the equity for that trade; if I enter the market with two currency pairs, then two trades, I will risk 1% for each trade, so as to always maintain an overall risk of 2%; if I enter with three currency pairs, then for the three trades, I will risk 0.66% (2% / 3= 0.66) for each trade, thus maintaining an overall risk always equal to 2% and so on.

It is good to know that with this technique is by no means appropriate to enter the market with too many currency pairs, you will see that operating on two pairs or at most three which have been well selected will be sufficient to obtain excellent results without complicating your life too much.

At this point, to calculate the right amount of capital to be used for each trade we just have to apply a simple mathematical calculation. Assuming that we have $10.000 in our account (equity) and knowing that the risk we can take for the trade is 2%, the calculation to be made is as follows:

$$10.000 / 100 = 100 \times 2 = 200\ \$$$

200$ is therefore equivalent to the capital to be used.
If on the contrary you want to enter the market with two pairs, then 2 trades, you have to

divide the 200 $ by 2, so 200 / 2 = 100 $.

As you can see, the formula to apply is very simple.

In my opinion, it is good to highlight the importance of always applying the same percentage of risk calculated based on the amount in your account, so it is essential that you understand that the percentage of risk - 2% - must always be calculated on the basis of the amount of your equity, whether it is growing or not.

Let's now look at how to **calculate the position sizing**, that is how to find the right amount of the size that will make us risk 2% once we enter the market. To do this, we must focus on the amount of money that corresponds to our 2%, so - following the example already mentioned - assuming that we have an equity of $ 10.000, 2% of 10.000 is $ 200, we will have to calculate the amount in lots to be used to enter the market and risk exactly $ 200.

To calculate the right amount of lots you need two elements: the first one is

the amount of money you are willing to lose (in our case 200 $); the second is the width of the stop loss expressed in number of pips, which in our strategy corresponds to the width of the NTZ.

These two elements are what it takes to calculate the size of the lot to enter the market with. Here is the formula:

$$\$ / PIPS = / 10 = ENTRY\ LOT$$

Let's look at an example assuming to have a stop loss equal to 16 pips:

$$200\$ \ / \ 16 \ \text{PIPS} = 12.5 \ / \ 10 = 1.25 \ \text{ENTRY LOT}$$

To enter the market and risk $200, you'll have to enter with 1.25 lots.

Let's now assume that we want to enter the market with 2 trades on two different pairs and that we still want to risk $200 all the time, which means that we have to risk $100 per currency pair. Now let's assume a stop loss of 13 pips for the first pair and a stop loss of 20 pips for the second; the calculation we will have to do will be:

$$100\$ \ / \ 13 \ \text{PIPS} = 7.69 \ / \ 10 = 0.76 \ \text{ENTRY LOT}$$

$$100\$ \ / \ 20 \ \text{PIPS} = 5/10 = 0.5 \ \text{ENTRY LOT}$$

So to have a total risk of $200 we will have to enter the first pair with a size of 0.76 lots and the second with a size of 0.5 lots.

These formulas represent simplified calculations that will help you to properly adjust the sizes so that you can always have the money you are willing to risk under control once you enter the market. However, keep in mind that for most platforms and especially MT4, there are several tools available from money managers that are capable of quickly and automatically calculating the percentage of risk and quantity of lots to be used.
You can find a lot of them and some of them even properly executed; the advice I can give you is to try some of them, choose the one you like most and learn how to use it in the most effective way, so that you can rely on it for your calculations.

Risk reward:

A fundamental element in money management is the **risk/reward**, i.e. the relationship between the risk taken per trade and the prospect of making a profit. This means that for each unit of risk that you are willing to take, you must have a return prospect equal to at least twice the loss, i.e. a ratio of 1:2, 1:3 or more.

This principle will allow us to easily overcome the sequences of negative trades, because it is clear that, assuming a risk/reward of 1:2, you can recover the loss of two negative trades with the closing of a positive trade. The same goes for a 1:3 ratio: one positive trade is enough to recover the loss of three negative trades.

The examples below are a good illustration.

Risk / Reward of 1:2

- 6 trades of which 3 are losses and 3 are profits
- 3 losses x -2% = -6%
- 3 profits x +4% = +12%

Final result: +6%

Risk / Reward of 1:3

- 10 trades of which 3 are losses and 7 are profits
- 3 losses x -2% = -6%
- 7 profits x +6% = 42%

Final result: +36%

Risk / Reward of 1:3

- 10 trades of which 5 are losses and 5 are profits
- 5 losses x -2% = -10%
- 5 profits x +6% = 30%

Final result: +20%

In fact, by evaluating these examples it is immediately understood why by adopting a risk/reward of 1:2 or 1:3, it is possible to maintain an advantage over negative trades sequences.
This is certainly the goal we must pursue when trading, but there is a small problem: the market is not predictable and does not always do what we want.

Indeed, when we open our trade, the only certainty we have is the amount of money we are willing to lose through the use of stop loss, but we can not determine how much the market is going to be affected beforehand and what levels of take profit it will attain, because the market does whatever it wants.

The only thing we can do is to apply a **trade management** that definitely aims to make us reach a good risk/reward when the trade starts moving on our side, but that at the same time protects the profits accrued up to that moment by keeping us safe in the event that the market turns against us going to hit the stop loss, thereby avoiding turning a successful trade into a loss, which happens very frequently when trading.

Trade management

Below are three trade management models. These are those that I apply in my operations and in my opinion are best suited to this strategy, that is those that in the medium/long term have proved to be the most performant

But first of all, a prerequisite is necessary.

All the models preview two trades per the day for the currency pair; if the first hits stop it can be entered again, but only from the opposite side of the NTZ. <u>You must never enter in the same direction twice</u>: if both trades hit a stop loss, our day of trading with that instrument is over and you will have to wait for the next day.

Model 1:

Model 1 has a trailing stop management: once the NTZ breakout has taken place, the position is left to run until it reaches TP 1, after which the stop loss is moved to breakeven so as not to risk any more loss. When TP 2 is reached, the stop loss is moved to TP 1; when TP 3 is reached, the stop loss is moved to TP 2 and so on.

In essence, to every new TP reached the stop loss is moved on to the previous TP until the market retraces and goes to hit our stop loss making us close the trade with the profit gained up to that moment.

An example is shown in the following chart:

Figure 56 GBP/JPY 2018/09/24

Figure 56 shows how, once TP 3 is reached, the market retraces and hits the stop loss positioned on TP 2, closing our trade with a risk/reward of 1:2.
Let's look at another example:

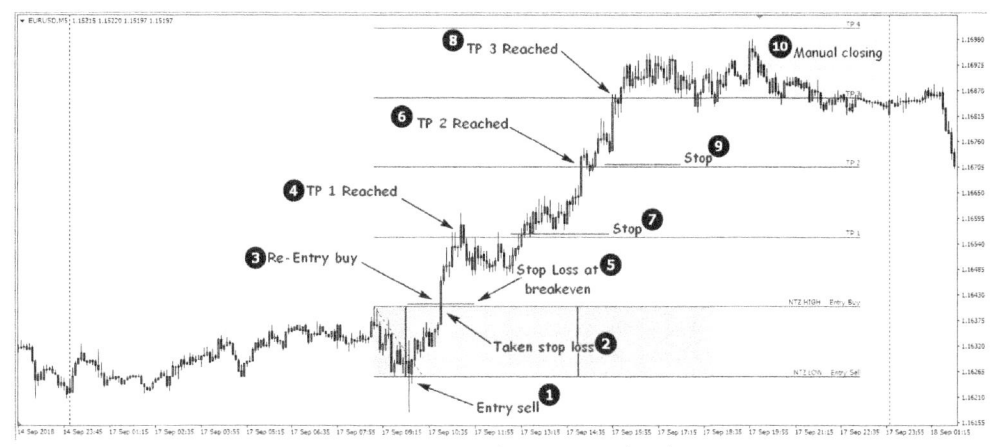

Figure 57 EUR/USD 2018/09/17

In Figure 57 we see a *short* entry goes into loss. In this case, it is allowed to enter again from the opposite side and start again with a new trade always managed using a trailing stop.

In this last chart we can see how, after the closing of London, due to the drastic reduction of the EUR/USD volumes, it goes into laterality and cannot reach either TP 4 or the stop loss positioned on TP 2. Well, in these cases it no longer makes sense to stay in the market because we risk carrying the trade overnight and since our strategy is an intraday strategy, once that time is reached a manual closure should be adopted, which in this case has allowed us to liquidate our position around TP 3 and take home a risk/reward of 1:3.

The advantage of this type of management is that on days with a wide range you can close trades with substantial risk/reward - even with ratios of 1:3, 1:4 and more - really exceptional results to be achieved with intraday strategies.

A downside of this model, however, could be to be thrown out too early because it can happen sometimes that, when the first TP is reached, the market goes to retest the level of entry by hitting the stop loss just moved to breakeven (Figure 58). Slightly bad though, because in these cases we will not be able to make a profit but fortunately we will not make a loss either.

Figure 58 EUR/USD 2018/09/20

Model 1 is simple to manage - because once you have entered the market it is only a matter of moving the stop loss every time a new level of take profit is reached - and it is recommended for those instruments that develop a good intraday directionality and that are not too volatile.

Model 2:

Model 2 has a partial exit with half of the position when TP 1 is reached and aims to reach TP 3 with the rest of the position. Therefore, when the TP 1 is reached, half of the position is closed and the stop loss is left unchanged; in this way, we immediately obtain two advantages.

The first one is related to the fact that if the market makes a pullback on our level of entry, we will not be thrown out (Figure 59) like it might happen with the model 1.

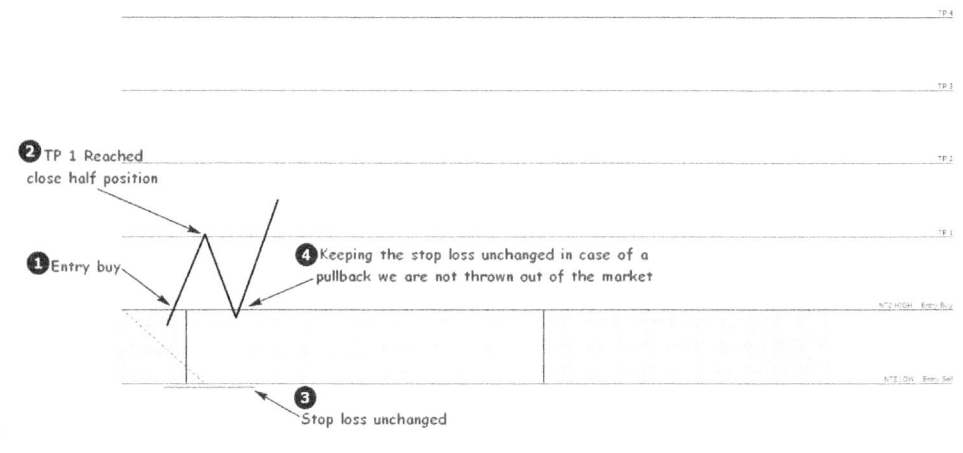

Figure 59

The second is related to the fact that, if the market turns against us and hits the stop loss, our trade would not close at a loss but to breakeven, because if we hypothetically entered with a risk of 2% and when we reached TP 1 we closed half of our position, in fact we would earn a gain of +1%. Consequently, by staying on with the remaining 1%, if the market went on to hit the stop loss we would generate with the second half of the position a loss equal to -1%, which added to +1% cashed previously would enable us to close the trade in parity (Figure 60).

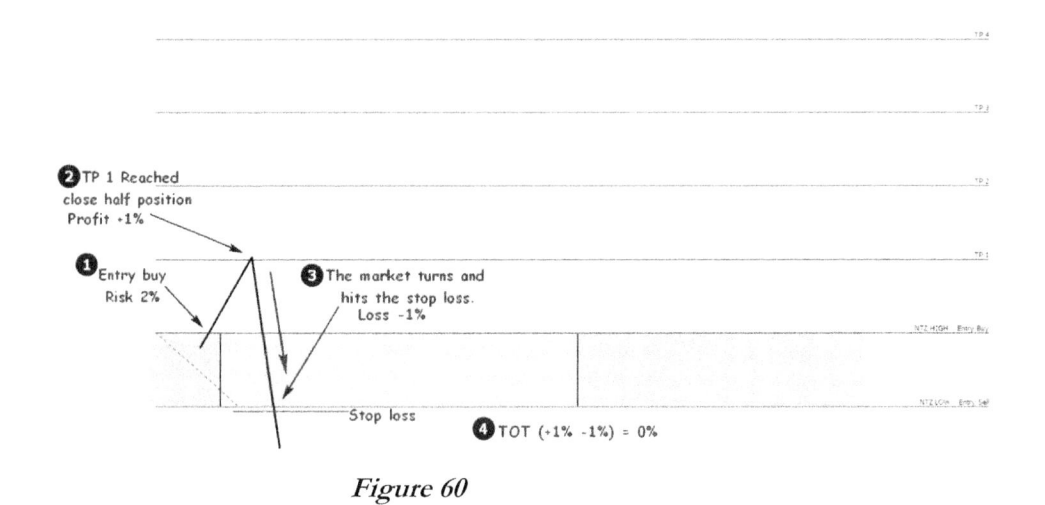

Figure 60

If we now exclude the hypothesis that the trade goes into stop loss, let's go ahead and see how to proceed with the management of the trade. We have therefore said that the market goes in our favor, the TP 1 has been reached, we have closed half of the position, cashed +1% and left the stop unchanged (Figure 61).

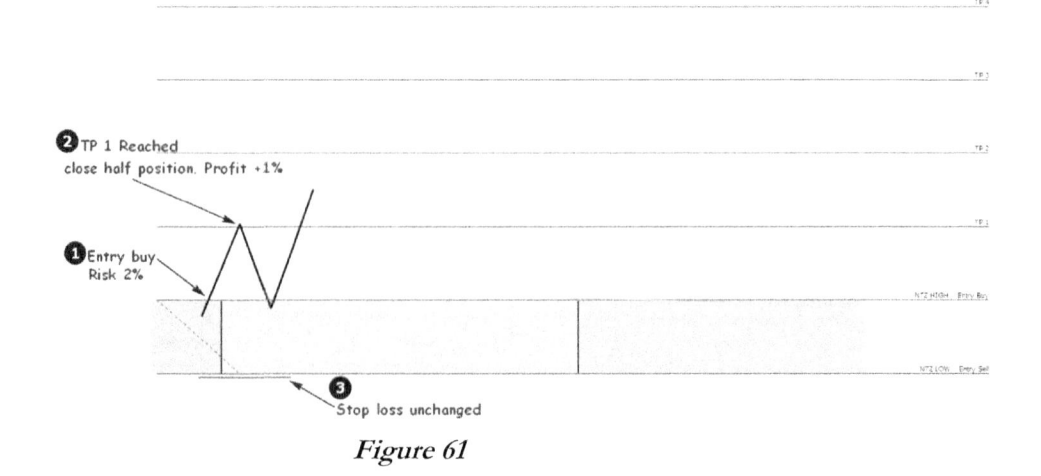

Figure 61

At this point, when the market reaches TP 2, we move the stop loss to TP 1 and keep it at that level until we reach the target set at TP 3 (Figure 62).

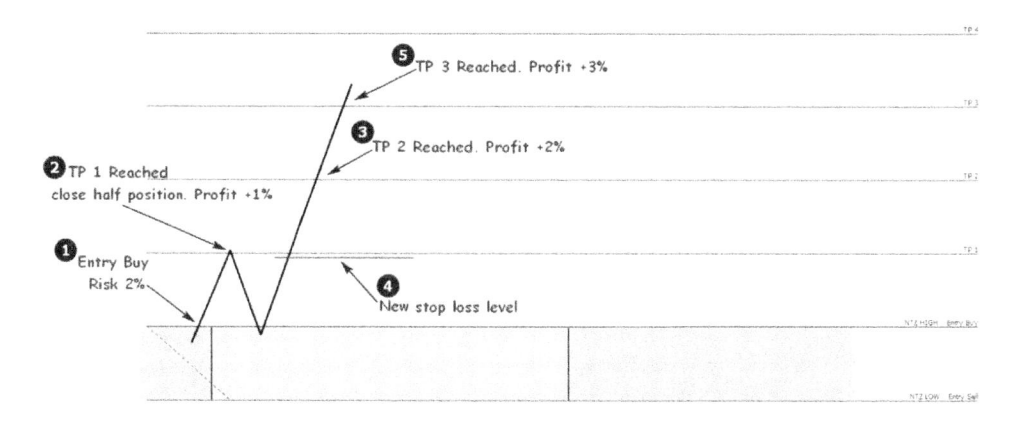

Figure 62

Why go straight out on TP 3?

Since this is a model that involves partial exit with half of the position, actually to obtain a risk/reward of 1:2 it is necessary to achieve the TP 3. This is because, if we enter as per the previous hypothesis with a risk of 2%, to have a return equal to 2 times the risk taken we would have to take home 4%. So with the first exit on TP 1 we collect +1% and with the second exit on TP 3 we collect +3%, which adds up to give us back our 4%.

Going beyond TP 3 will be aspiring for a profit higher than a risk/reward of 1:2 and this would significantly reduce the chances of success of model 2, because - contrary to what you might think - the further away the target is from the entry point the lower the chances of it being taken. Therefore I can say with certainty that, after having carried out numerous backtests on various instruments, the TP 3 has turned out to be the most balanced target.

Let's now look at some real situations on the charts:

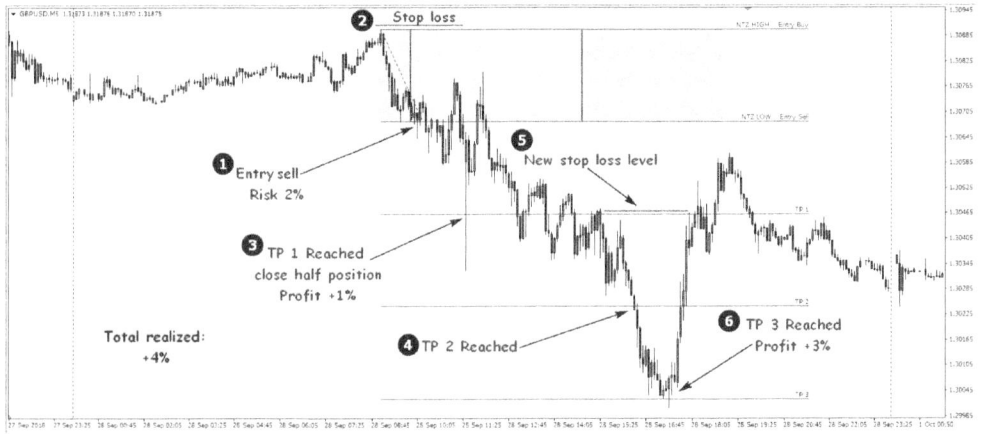

Figure 63 GBP/USD 2018/09/28

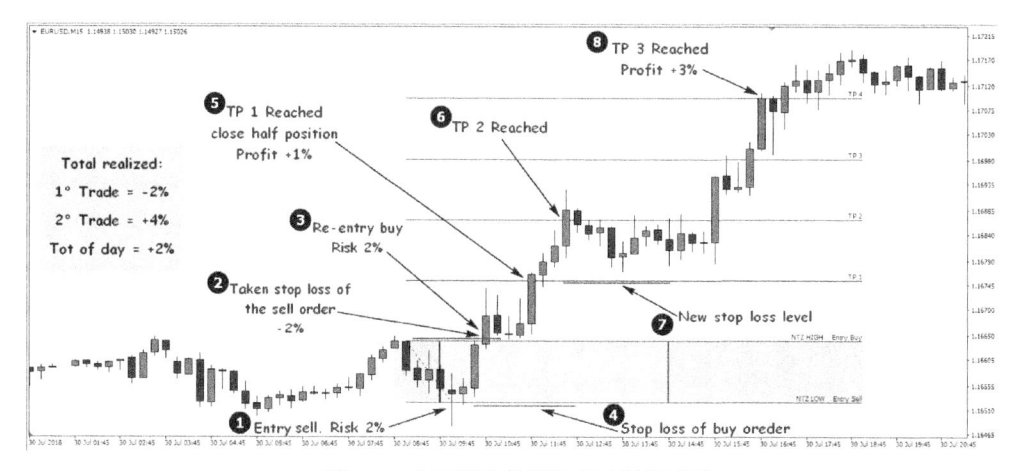

Figure 64 EUR/USD 2018/07/30

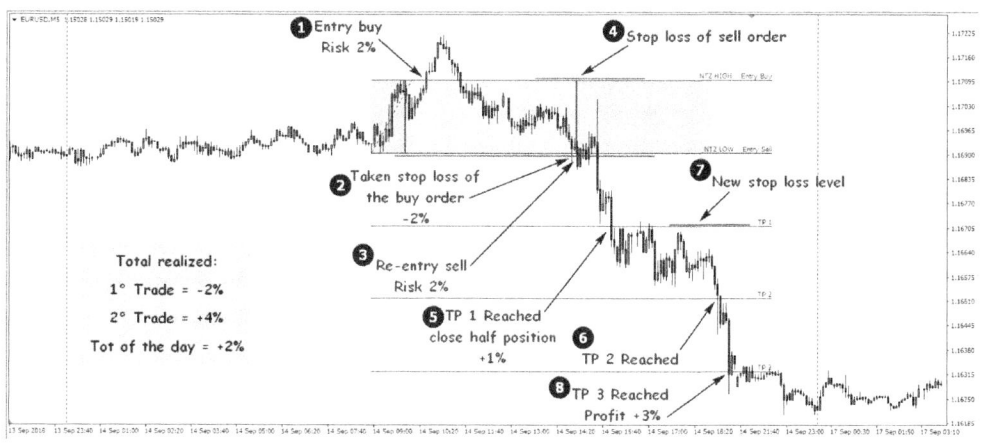

Figure 65 EUR/USD 2018/09/14

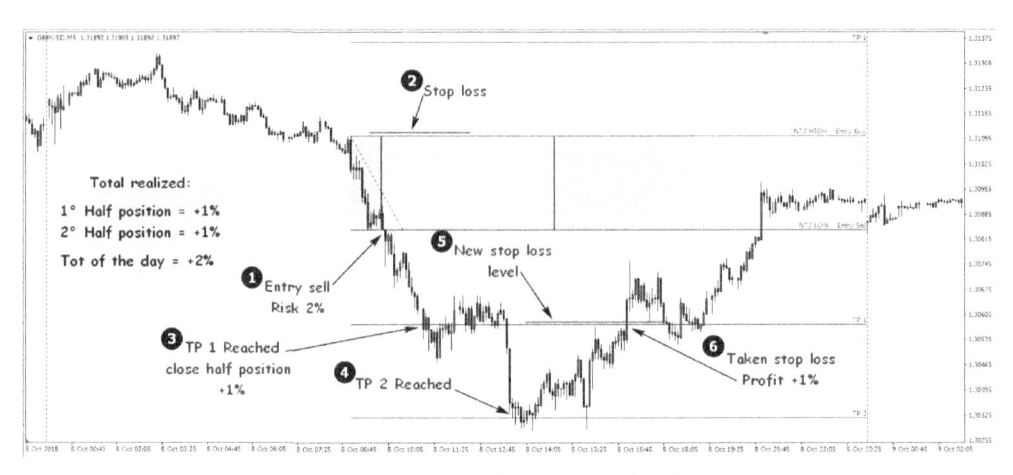

Figure 66 GBP/USD 2018/10/08

Model 2 has a well-balanced management solution, because its implementation ensures that we are safe from the moment we reach TP 1, while from the moment we reach TP 2 it guarantees a gain equal to the risk taken and with TP 3 we bring home a satisfactory 1:2.

It is however recommended for instruments that have the tendency to reverse the trend during the sessions and have good intraday movement fluctuations.

Model 3:

Model 3 has a simpler management than the previous model, since it does not involve a partial exit or a trailing stop. The fixed target set on the TP 2 is inserted and the stop loss is moved only once to be positioned at breakeven when the TP 1 is reached; after that the only thing left to do is to wait for the target on the TP 2 to be reached.

Let's see some examples below:

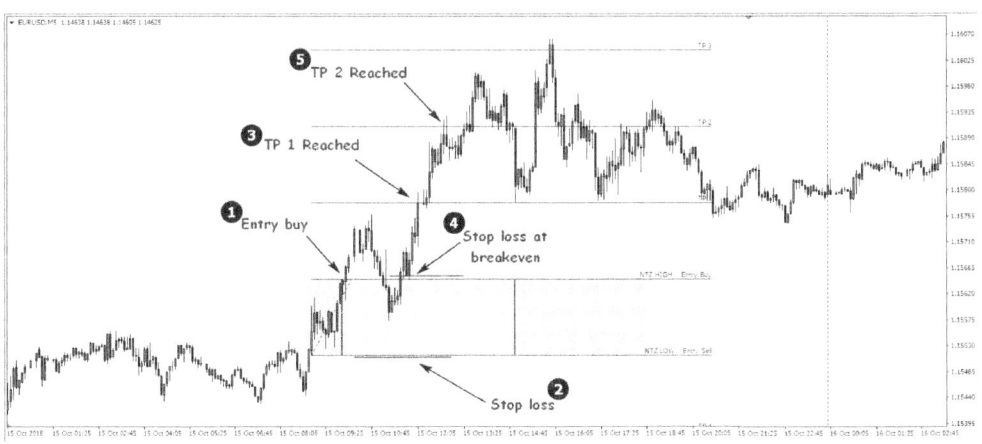

Figure 67 EUR/USD 2018/10/15

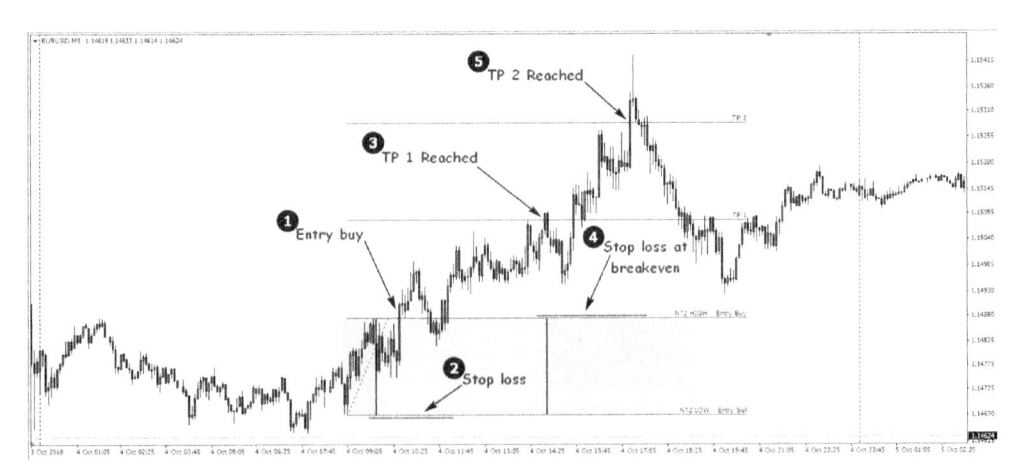

Figure 68 EUR/USD 2018/10/04

In the chart below two consecutive days are shown with three trades executed of which one hit stop loss, the simulation was made with a risk equal to 2% per trade:

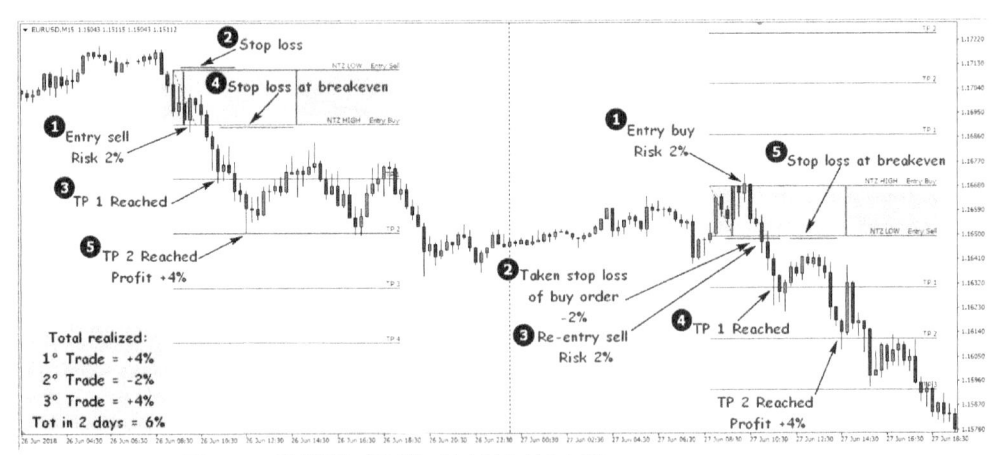

Figure 69 EUR/USD 2018/06/26-27

This model of management, besides being simple, turns out to be very effective for those currency pairs that do not have very wide intraday ranges and often have the tendency to invert course passing from *long* to *short* movements and vice versa during the same session, since it protects us from the risk taken from the attainment of the TP 1 and the target on the TP 2 is rather easily reachable guaranteeing an appreciable risk/reward of 1:2.

How to handle the second pending order

As stated at the beginning of the previous Chapter, all models have two trades a day per currency pair. If the first one hits stop loss, you can enter again but only from the opposite side of the NTZ (<u>you should never enter twice in the same direction</u>). If both trades hit stop loss, our trading day on that instrument is over and you have to wait until the next day.

Since there are two pending orders that are placed on the platform just before the opening of London, in addition to the rules mentioned above, it is appropriate to understand how it is necessary to manage the second order once you have entered the market with the first.

To show you this, I have decided to divide the incidences that can occur into three main variants, so that you can understand each situation.

I must say that the first rule to keep in mind is that, if you are on target with the first trade, the second pending order must be canceled, because it is useless to make the second trade and risk taking a stop loss when we have already made a profit with the first trade:

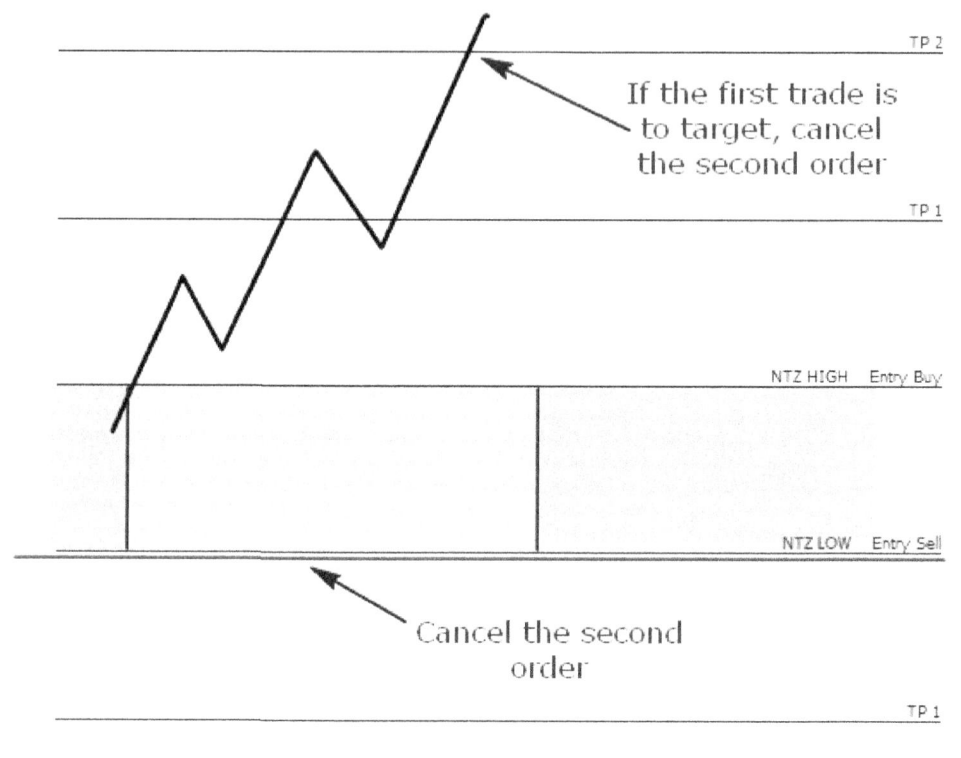

Figure 70

Having said that, let's look at the possible variants below.

Variant A

If we enter the market with the first trade and the TP 1 is not reached, the market turns and hits the stop loss, the second order must be kept on the platform:

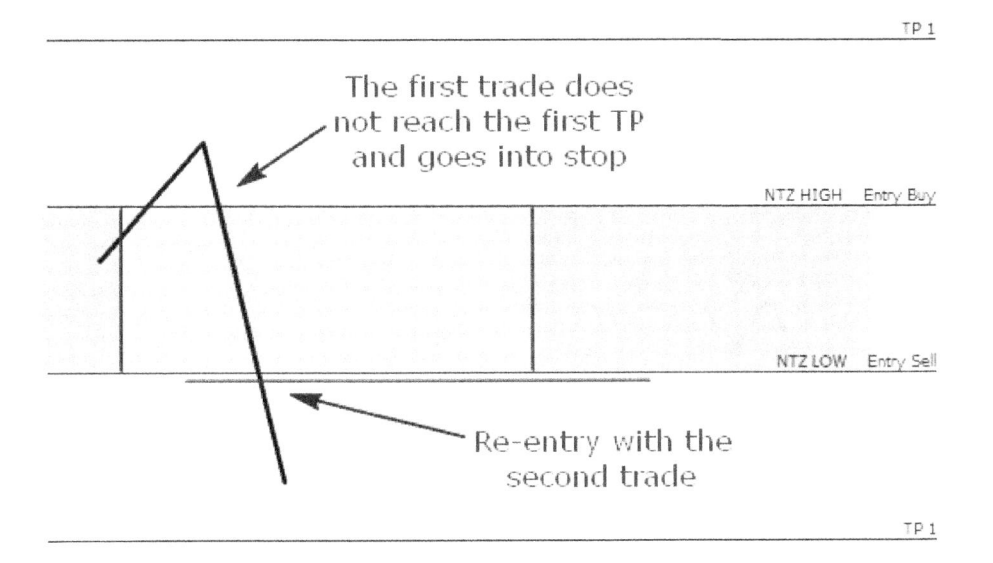

Figure 71

Variant B

If we enter the market with the first trade, the TP 1 is reached and the market changes direction, the second order should be kept on the platform as *long* as we are in the peach box or in the first part of the turquoise box:

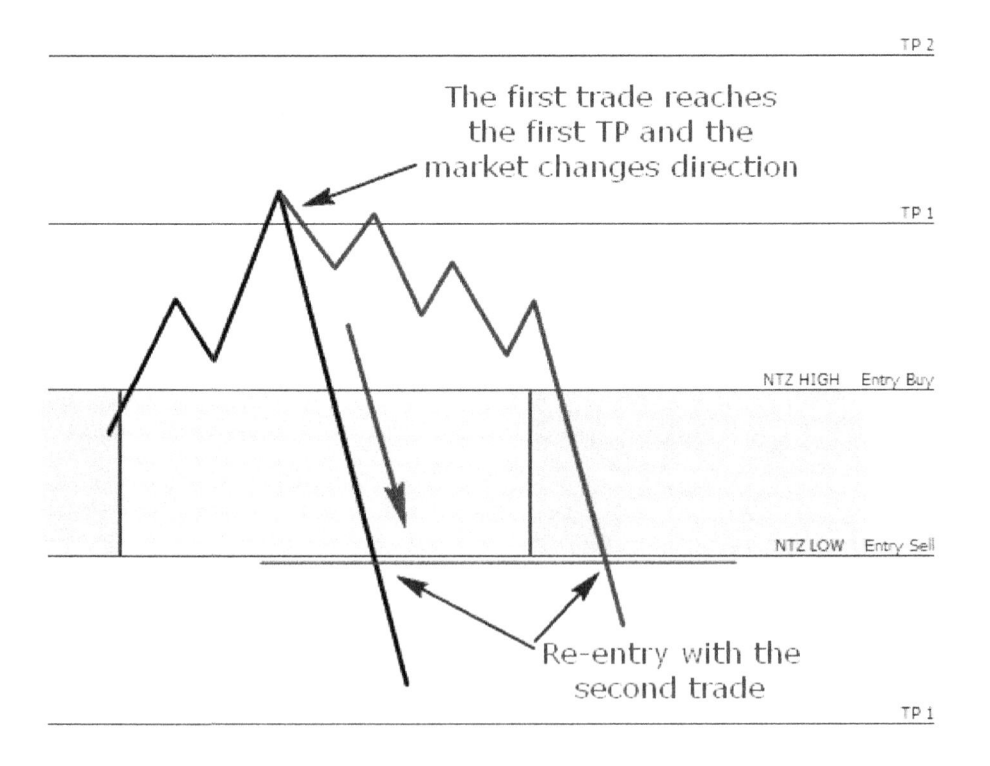

Figure 72

Variant C

If we enter the market with the first trade, the second TP is reached and the market changes direction, the second order should be kept on the platform as *long* as we are in the peach box or in the first part of the turquoise box:

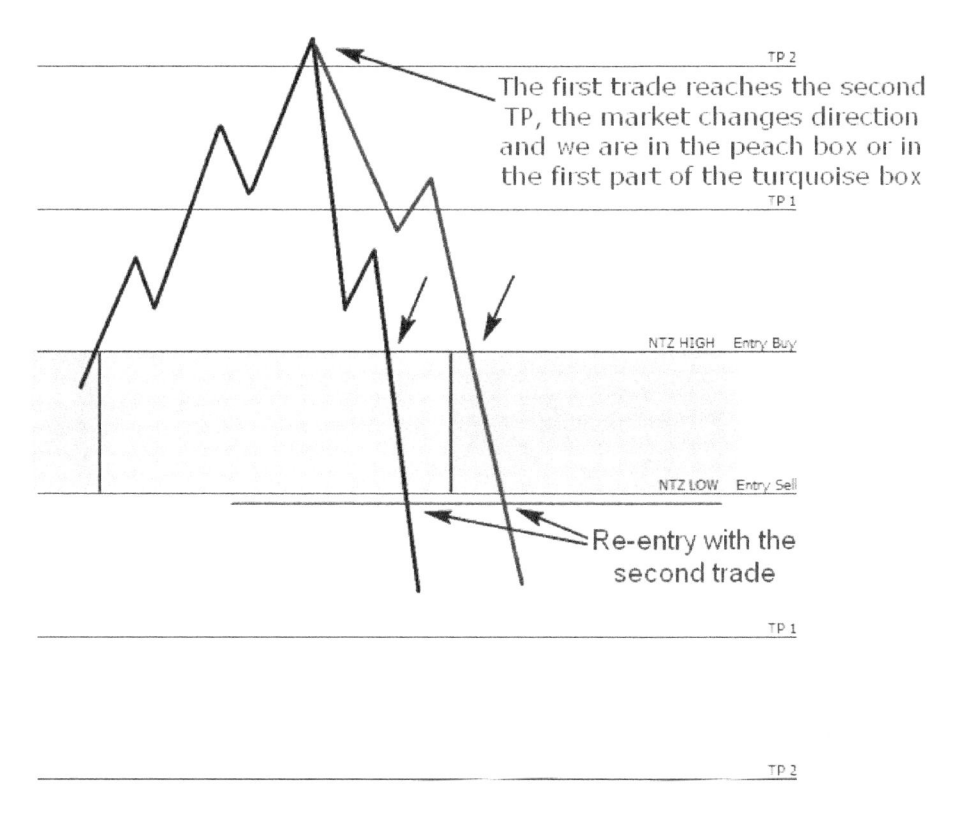

Figure 73

For illustrative purposes, only examples in the *long* direction are given; of course the subject of variants A, B and C is mirrored in the case where the first trade is *short*.

Another case that may occur, albeit very rarely (and that is why it was deliberately not catalogued as a variant), is when the price remains within the NTZ area for much of the session without picking up our pending orders. Well, in this case, once you arrive at the top of the turquoise box, you need to cancel both orders because it is evident that we are facing a market congestion and it is advisable to avoid them being picked when it is too late.

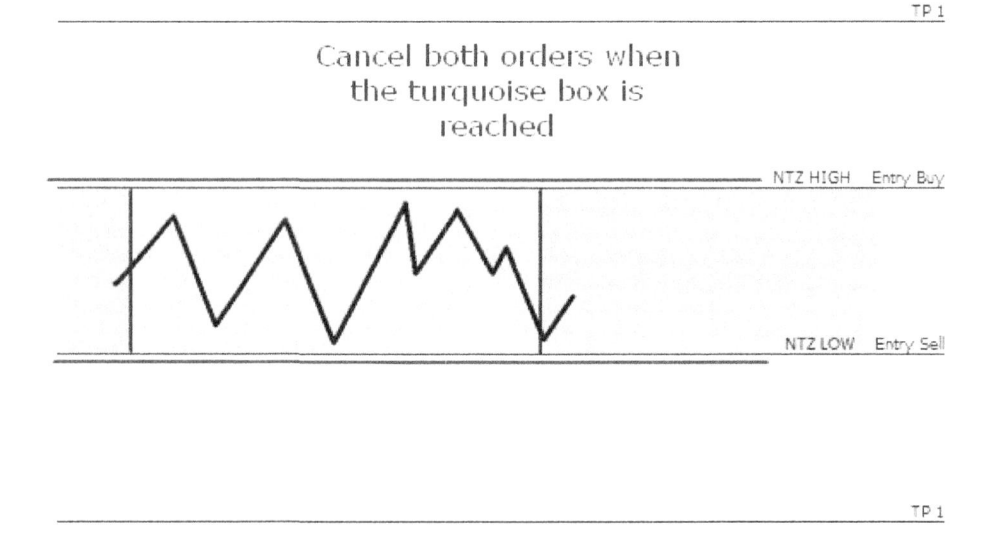

Figure 74

Keep in mind, furthermore, that if you trade more than one currency pair - for example three or four - to avoid excessive-exporting you can also decide to make only one trade per day per instrument. In this case, as soon as the first order is executed, all you have to do is cancel the second order and focus on the relevant trade management model.

The importance of backtesting

Finding the right currency pair is of paramount importance for the proper implementation of the strategy. It is recommended that you create a watchlist of seven or eight changes to follow by recording the performance of each, in order to have a record and a statistical archive that enables you to assess based on the results obtained, which model of trade management is most appropriate to apply to each individual currency pair.

It is important to keep a record of our entire watchlist so that we can analyze it statistically: the greater the data we collect on the market and on our operations, the more we expand our knowledge and the greater the chances of success.

I would advise you to initially focus only on one exchange rate (such as EUR/USD, which is actually the most traded currency pair and offers a good balance between volatility and directionality of movements): start by analyzing the past by first applying MODEL 1, then MODEL 2 and finally MODEL 3 of trade management; record each of their performances in a diary. The model which turns out to be the most appropriate will be the one you should start to trade with.

Only later, when you are more familiar with the method, will you be able to add more currency pairs. But do not be in a hurry: it is better to start with a single well analyzed instrument than with several instruments which have been analyzed in a rush and perhaps not in depth.

Remember that in trading the bulk of the work is done during backtesting, studying and re-studying historical data, the moment of clicking to *buy* or *sell* is just the final act of a great planning strategy.

Final notes

We have come to the end of this book, which contains years of analysis, studies and research aimed at creating a solid operating method, a method that can be applied by anyone regardless of their personality, because it is a method that bases revenue on non-discretionary criteria and because of this very reason, it does not require special skills or applications.

In this book we have carefully analyzed all the information as much as possible to ensure it is easy to understand, while we have avoided using a language that is too technical in order to extrapolate only the information that can really be useful to start a profitable path in the currency market.

This is a method specifically for Forex, a reliable method, tested with real transactions and which has proven to be a balanced and effective method. However, I would like to stress that it is essential to follow every rule involved while using it, because - remember - even the most perfect of strategies can be wasted and produce losses when used by people without discipline.

Regardless of these statements, before investing your money you will still have to study this method in depth, you will need to gain the right confidence and remember that to be successful you need passion, dedication, discipline and a lot of time needs to be spent so you can be perfect.

Success in the currency market is within everyone's reach, but only a few will actually achieve it, because not everyone has the tenacity to carry out such a challenging project.

Be wary of those who offer you the infallible method: whatever the price requested and whatever the profit promised, the infallible method does not exist. Only research, commitment and dedication leads to success.

Respect the method. Do not switch from one method to another.

Always use stop losses... they are your lifeline!

Record all your trades in a trading diary: NTZ range, income, expenses, trade management model applied, second order management variant pending, how the market evolved on that day... this is the only way you will gain knowledge of recurring price dynamics.

Another very important thing is the choice of your broker: it is essential that it is reliable, enrolled in the supervisory commissions of various countries, well capitalized and known in the world. Make sure that it is not based in some tax haven, that it offers good platforms and that it is fast in executing; moreover, it is important that it has low spreads.

When choosing a broker, it is essential to also check the quality of customer service and make sure it is efficient: before opening a real account, simply call for assistance for a test and get an explanation on all the information you need. The broker must provide you with confidence and security. Having said that, I can only say goodbye and wish you success in trading!

Gabriele Fabris

Resources:

Watch the video on my YouTube channel, it will help you set up *Fibonacci* as described in the "*Fibonacci tips*" Chapter on page 69:

https://youtu.be/AV053E7QBII

If you want to stay updated on my activities and receive tips and news on strategy, follow me on my social media pages! You will find all the information you need to stay informed and get the most out of your trading.

If you have any questions or doubts, do not hesitate to contact our customer support team at **thepriceintime@gmail.com**, they will be always at your disposal to help you and answer your questions.

@gabry_trader_fx

The Price In Time Forex Strategy

In this book, I have described a very effective strategy, the result of many years of study and experience in financial markets, knowledge that I wanted to share with the ambition that you too can make your trading simple and profitable. From personal experience, I know that, despite the step-by-step description of the strategy and being ready to use, its application is not easy, and doubts and fears quickly take over.

To help you take the next step in the application of this strategy and to provide you with greater support for the simple modified Fibonacci levels, I have specially created the **"NTZ Box Breakout"** indicator, a specific tool for the MT4 platform that will help you apply the strategy quickly and effectively.

The indicator will automatically create colored boxes of the various sessions and the extensions of the "Take Profit levels", if the Asian session and the "NTZ area" do not meet the correct parameters, the boxes will turn red indicating that the currency pair will not be suitable for trade. In addition, the money manager will calculate the size of the positions. In practice, once installed, you will not have to worry about doing everything manually but you can focus only on managing the trades, making your operation more fluid and faster.

That being said, I believe that the real power of this indicator is the speed that you can have in analyzing historical data for backtesting, because it is possible to view the "NTZ Boxes" and "Take Profit levels" even for past days and recording past performance becomes very immediate.

In the following pages, I have integrated the guide to its use so that you can see what its features are.

NTZ BOX BREAKOUT
User's guide for MT4

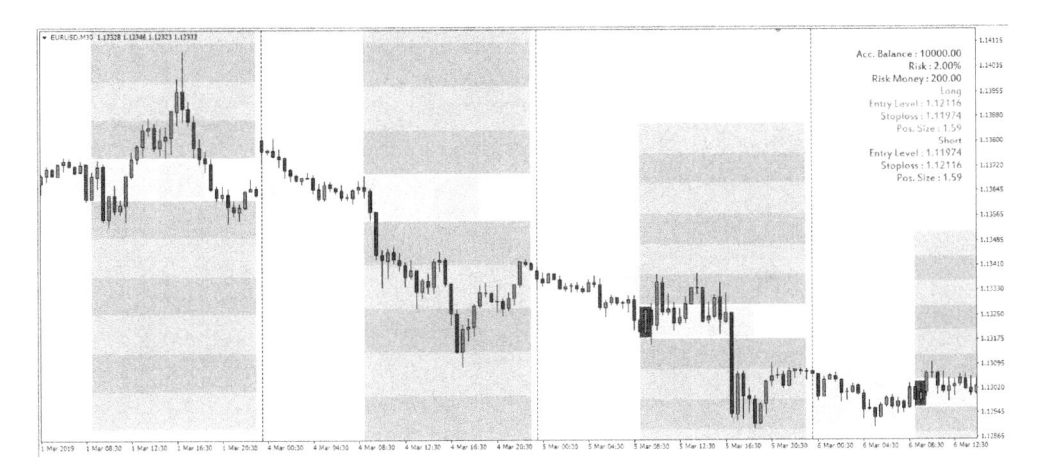

This indicator has been specially developed to complement **The Price in Time** strategy.

The **NTZ BOX BREAKOUT** indicator automatically creates:

- **The Day separators**
- The **No Trading Zone** divided with the **Green Box**, the **Peach Box** and the **Turqoise Box**
- Extensions of the *long* and *short* **Take Profit** levels
- The **Yellow Box** to display the range of the Asian session
- The **Money Manager** for a perfect **Position Sizing** calculated on your risk percentage

Using the **NTZ BOX** indicator will enable you to have your trading plan ready when London opens and thanks to the history display function you can perform your backtests by quickly and accurately **applying the Trade Management Models 1-2-3** described in **The Price in Time** strategy.

Customize the first 3 parameters

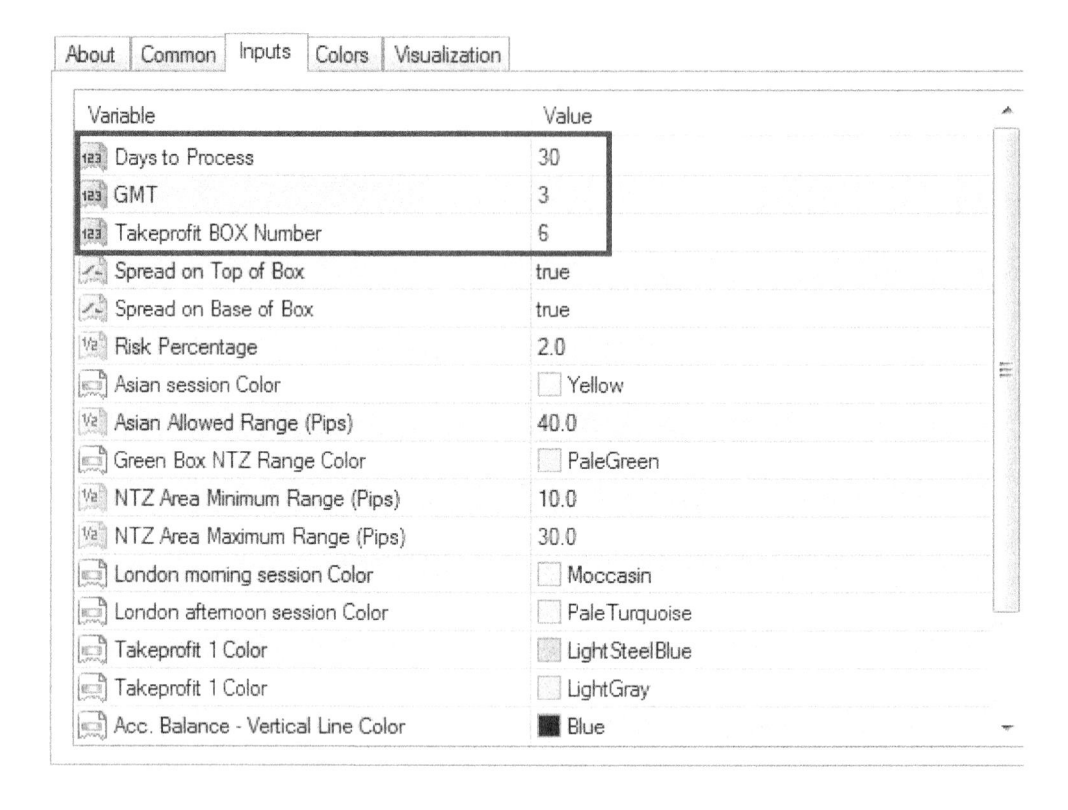

Variable	Value
Days to Process	30
GMT	3
Takeprofit BOX Number	6
Spread on Top of Box	true
Spread on Base of Box	true
Risk Percentage	2.0
Asian session Color	Yellow
Asian Allowed Range (Pips)	40.0
Green Box NTZ Range Color	PaleGreen
NTZ Area Minimum Range (Pips)	10.0
NTZ Area Maximum Range (Pips)	30.0
London morning session Color	Moccasin
London afternoon session Color	PaleTurquoise
Takeprofit 1 Color	LightSteelBlue
Takeprofit 1 Color	LightGray
Acc. Balance - Vertical Line Color	Blue

Days to Process: Select the number of days you want them to be processed and analyze what the market has done in the past days.

GMT: Select the GMT of your Broker and the indicator will automatically synchronize the Boxes.

Take Profit Number: Choose the number of Take Profits you want to display on the chart.

Viewing the Spread

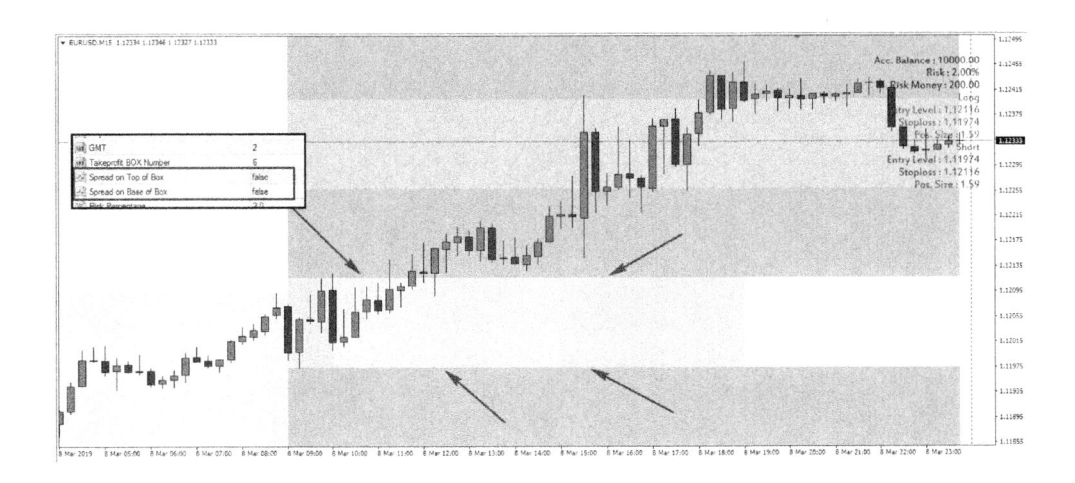

You can choose to view the spread at the ends of the NTZ area in order to <u>optimize your revenue by placing orders after the spread</u>.

Variable	Value
Days to Process	30
GMT	2
Takeprofit BOX Number	6
Spread on Top of Box	true
Spread on Base of Box	true
Risk Percentage	2.0

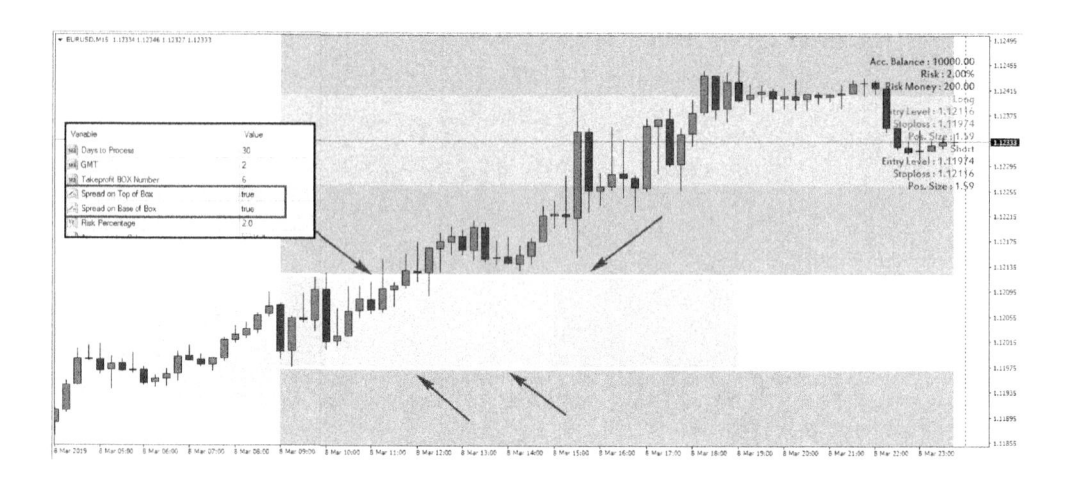

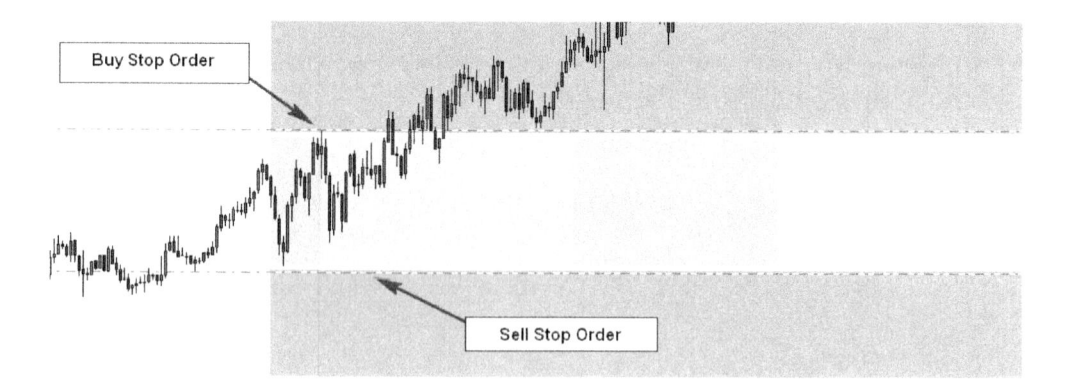

Money Manager

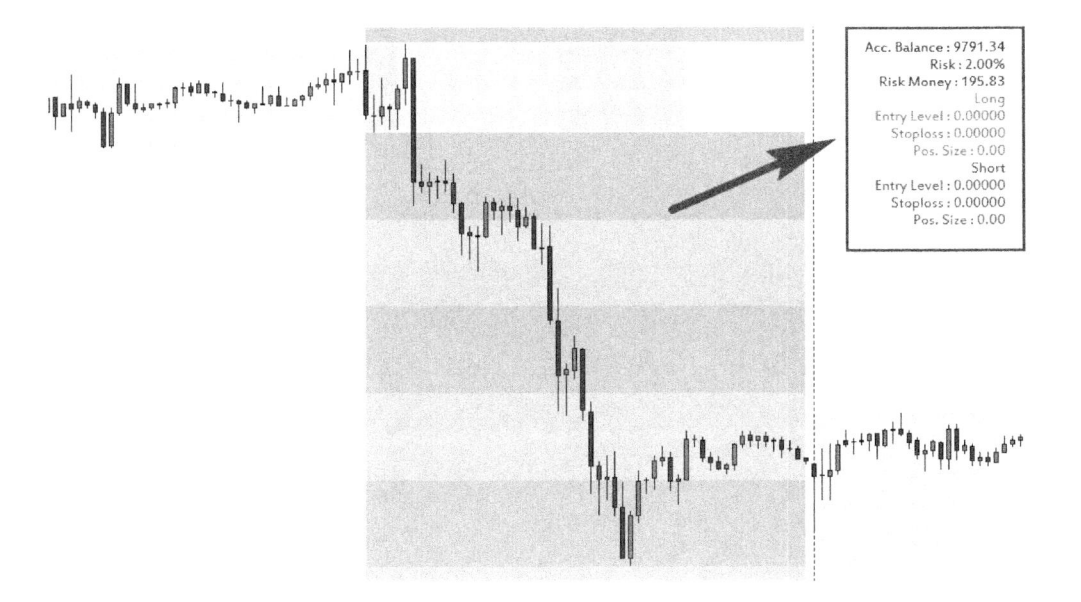

Enter your risk percentage and the Money Manager will give you the values described below:

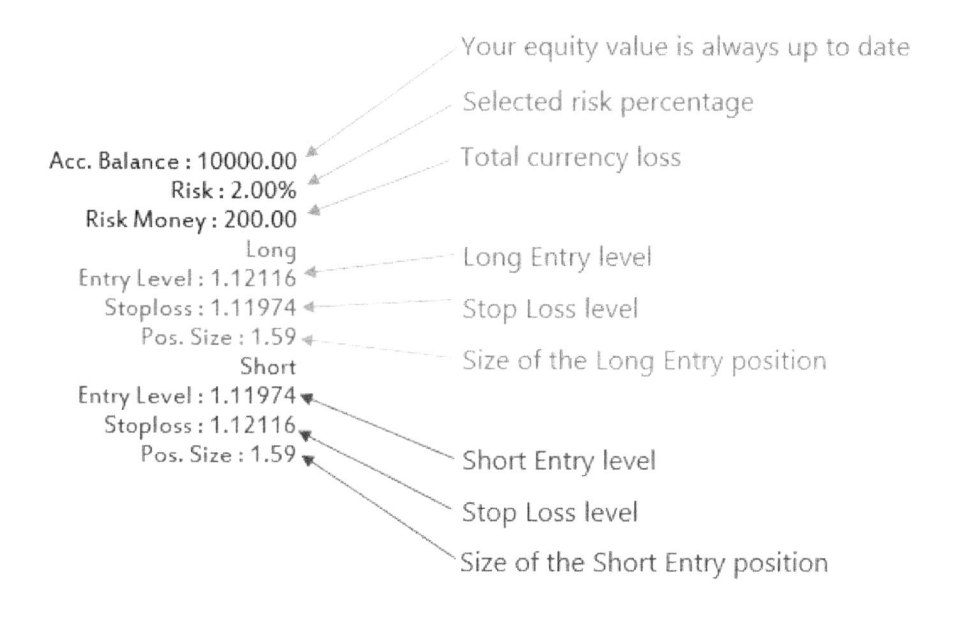

Acc. Balance : 10000.00 — Your equity value is always up to date
Risk : 2.00% — Selected risk percentage
Risk Money : 200.00 — Total currency loss

Long
Entry Level : 1.12116 — Long Entry level
Stoploss : 1.11974 — Stop Loss level
Pos. Size : 1.59 — Size of the Long Entry position

Short
Entry Level : 1.11974
Stoploss : 1.12116
Pos. Size : 1.59 — Short Entry level
— Stop Loss level
— Size of the Short Entry position

Box of the Asian session

Asian Session Color:
Choose the color of the Asian session box.

Asian Allowed Range (Pips):
The Asian session box is set to a maximum range of 40 pips, however, you can change this value in order to better adapt the **NTZ BOX** indicator to the volatility of each currency pair.

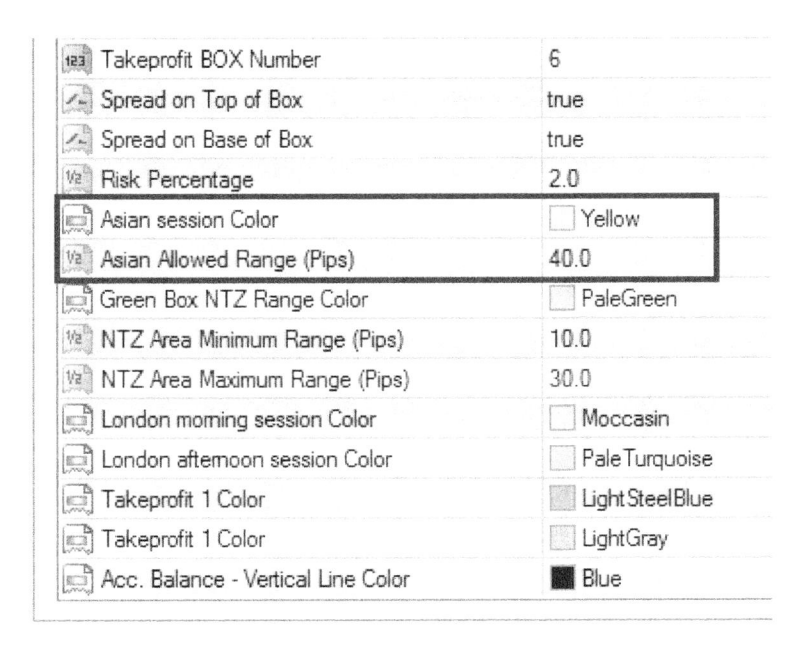

Takeprofit BOX Number	6
Spread on Top of Box	true
Spread on Base of Box	true
Risk Percentage	2.0
Asian session Color	Yellow
Asian Allowed Range (Pips)	40.0
Green Box NTZ Range Color	PaleGreen
NTZ Area Minimum Range (Pips)	10.0
NTZ Area Maximum Range (Pips)	30.0
London morning session Color	Moccasin
London afternoon session Color	PaleTurquoise
Takeprofit 1 Color	LightSteelBlue
Takeprofit 1 Color	LightGray
Acc. Balance - Vertical Line Color	Blue

If the price movement of the Asian session is too big and exceeds 40 pips (or the maximum value we have chosen) the box becomes red, warning us that it is not advisable to trade.

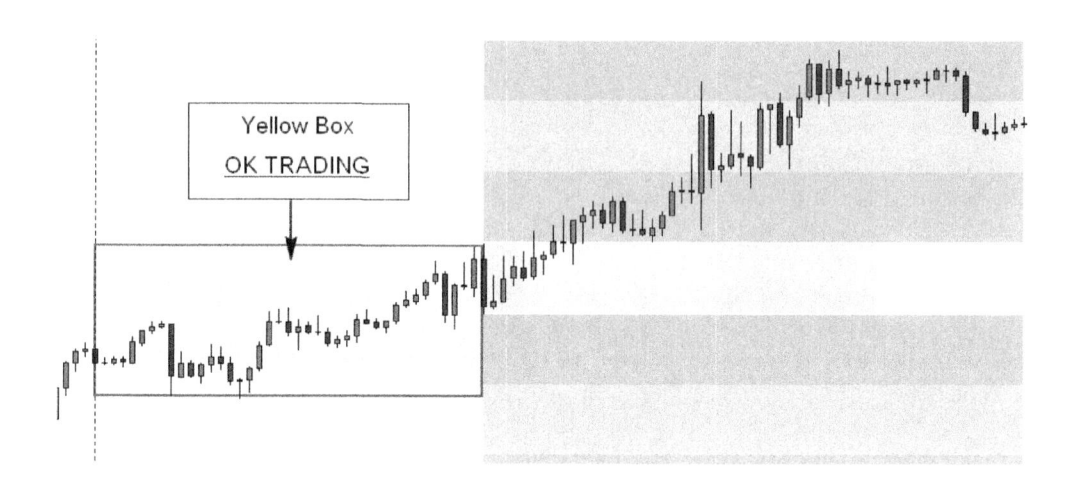

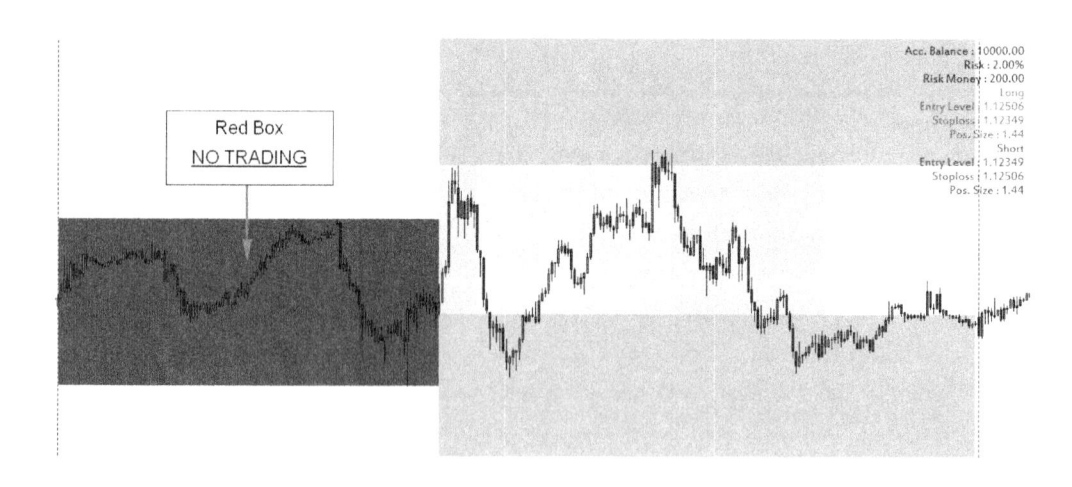

Yellow Box
OK TRADING

Red Box
NO TRADING

Green Box (NTZ Range)

Variable	Value
Spread on Top of Box	true
Spread on Base of Box	true
Risk Percentage	2.0
Asian session Color	Yellow
Asian Allowed Range (Pips)	40.0
Green Box NTZ Range Color	**PaleGreen**
NTZ Area Minimum Range (Pips)	**10.0**
NTZ Area Maximum Range (Pips)	**30.0**
London morning session Color	Moccasin
London afternoon session Color	PaleTurquoise
Takeprofit 1 Color	LightSteelBlue
Takeprofit 1 Color	LightGray
Acc. Balance - Vertical Line Color	Blue

Green Box NTZ Range Color:
It is possible to customize the color of the green box.

NTZ Area Minimum Range (Pips):
It is possible to change the minimum value of the NTZ area range.

NTZ Area Maximum Range (Pips):
It is possible to change the maximum value of the NTZ area range.

The values of the green box range (NTZ Area) are preset at 10 and 30 pips in relation to what is described in the **The Price in Time** strategy; however, it is possible to modify these values in order to better adapt the **NTZ BOX** indicator to the volatility of each single currency pair.

If an NTZ area with a range greater or lesser to the preset values is created the green box becomes red warning us that it is not advisable to trade.

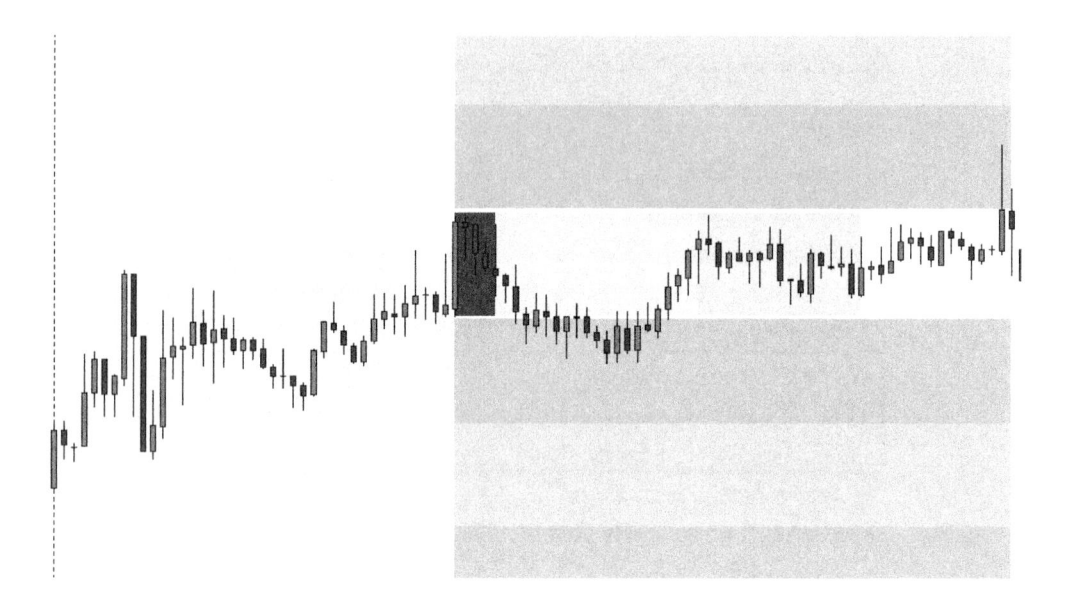

Customize the appearance of the indicator

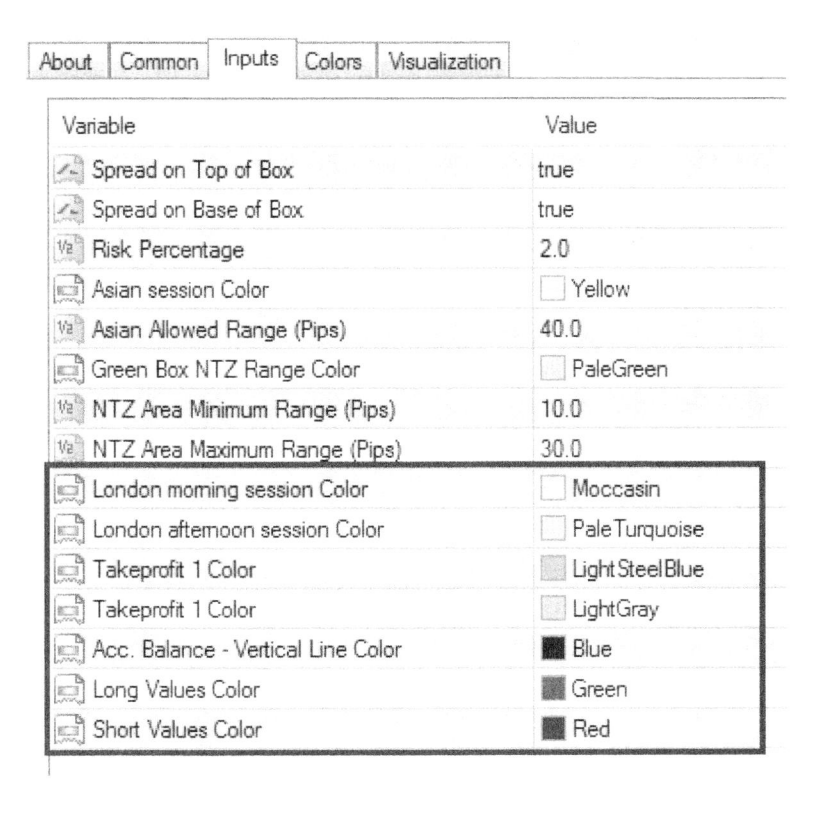

Variable	Value
Spread on Top of Box	true
Spread on Base of Box	true
Risk Percentage	2.0
Asian session Color	Yellow
Asian Allowed Range (Pips)	40.0
Green Box NTZ Range Color	PaleGreen
NTZ Area Minimum Range (Pips)	10.0
NTZ Area Maximum Range (Pips)	30.0
London morning session Color	Moccasin
London afternoon session Color	PaleTurquoise
Takeprofit 1 Color	LightSteelBlue
Takeprofit 1 Color	LightGray
Acc. Balance - Vertical Line Color	Blue
Long Values Color	Green
Short Values Color	Red

It is possible to change the colours of NTZ boxes, Take Profit boxes and Money Manager for a completely personalized visual impact.

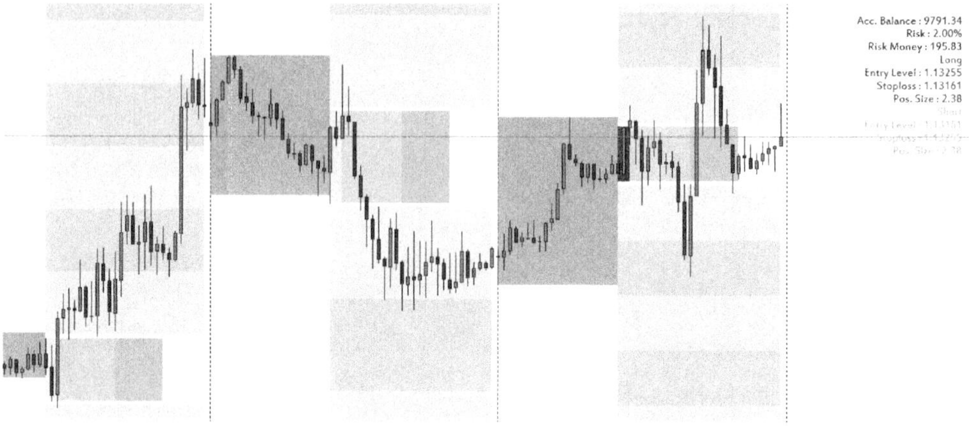
Acc. Balance : 9791.34
Risk : 2.00%
Risk Money : 195.83
Long
Entry Level : 1.13255
Stoploss : 1.13161
Pos. Size : 2.38

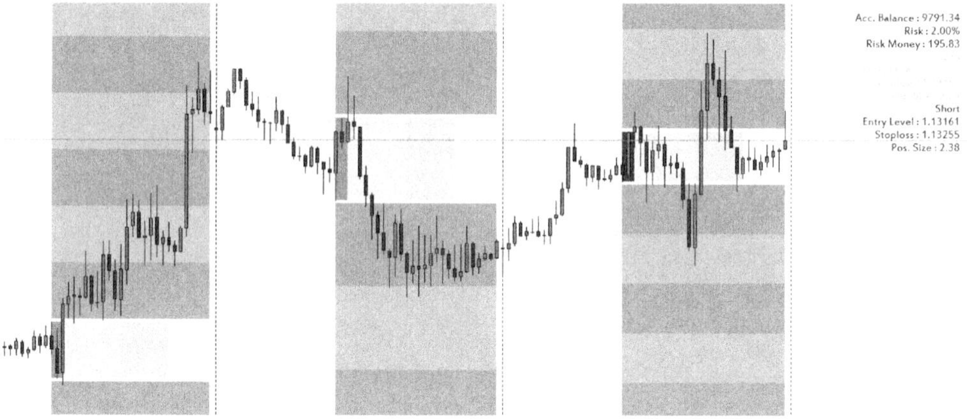
Acc. Balance : 9791.34
Risk : 2.00%
Risk Money : 195.83
Short
Entry Level : 1.13161
Stoploss : 1.13255
Pos. Size : 2.38

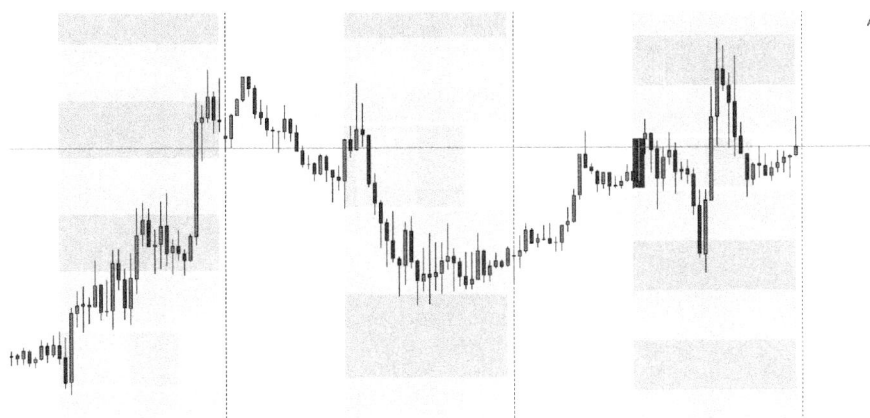

If you are interested in purchasing the **"NTZ Box Breakout"** indicator, you can find it on the MQL5 market website at **www.mql5.com** by simply typing the indicator name in the search bar. Alternatively, you can find it using Google by typing the following link:

https://www.mql5.com/en/market/product/38244

This link will take you directly to the product page where you can purchase and download it.

Thank you for purchasing my book. I hope you have spent a pleasant time immersed in reading and that you have discovered new and interesting ideas.

As an author, reviews are crucial to me and the success of the book. They help to reach a wider audience and improve my future writings. Also, they are very helpful for other readers who are looking for an interesting and well-written book.

I just ask for a few minutes of your time to leave an honest review on Amazon. I assure you that your opinion will be greatly appreciated and will be very helpful for other readers who are interested in discovering this book.

Once again, thank you for purchasing my book. I am glad to know what you think.

Gabriele Fabris

@gabry_trader_fx

The Price In Time Forex Strategy

Printed in Great Britain
by Amazon